BUSINESS ISSUES, COMPETITION AND ENTREPRENEURSHIP

LARGE PARTNERSHIPS

GROWTH TRENDS AND IRS CHALLENGES

BUSINESS ISSUES, COMPETITION AND ENTREPRENEURSHIP

Additional books in this series can be found on Nova's website under the Series tab.

Additional e-books in this series can be found on Nova's website under the e-book tab.

BUSINESS ISSUES, COMPETITION AND ENTREPRENEURSHIP

LARGE PARTNERSHIPS

GROWTH TRENDS AND IRS CHALLENGES

FRANCIS E. STEPHENS
EDITOR

NOVINKA
New York

Library of Congress Cataloging-in-Publication Data

ISBN: 978-1-63463-725-1

Published by Nova Science Publishers, Inc. † New York

CONTENTS

PREFACE

The number of large partnerships has more than tripled to 10,099 from tax year 2002 to 2011. Almost two-thirds of large partnerships had more than 1,000 direct and indirect partners, had six or more tiers and/or self reported being in the finance and insurance sector, with many being investment funds. The Internal Revenue Service (IRS) audits few large partnerships. Most audits resulted in no change to the partnership's return and the aggregate change was small. Although internal control standards call for information about effective resource use, IRS has not defined what constitutes a large partnership and does not have codes to track these audits. According to IRS auditors, the audit results may be due to challenges such as finding the sources of income within multiple tiers while meeting the administrative tasks required by the Tax Equity and Fiscal Responsibility Act of 1982 (TEFRA) within specified time frames. This book determines what IRS knows about the number and characteristics of large partnerships; assesses IRS's ability to audit them; and also assess IRS's efforts to address the audit challenges.

Chapter 1 - More businesses are organizing as partnerships while fewer are C corporations. Unlike C corporations, partnerships do not pay income taxes but pass on income and losses to their partners. Large partnerships (those GAO defined as having $100 million or more in assets and 100 or more direct and indirect partners) are growing in number and have complex structures. Some partnerships create tiers of partnerships with hundreds of thousands of partners. Tiered large partnerships are challenging for IRS to audit because tracing income through the tiers to the ultimate partners is complex.

GAO was asked to assess IRS's ability to audit large partnerships. GAO's objectives include: 1) determine what IRS knows about the number and characteristics of large partnerships, 2) assess IRS's ability to audit them, and

3) assess IRS's efforts to address the audit challenges. GAO analyzed IRS data from 2002 to 2011 and IRS audit documentation, interviewed IRS officials, met with IRS auditors in six focus groups, and interviewed private sector tax lawyers knowledgeable about partnerships.

Chapter 2 - In recent years, the number of businesses organized as partnerships has increased significantly, rising 47 percent between tax years 2002 and 2011. In tax year 2011, nearly 3.3 million partnerships accounted for $20.6 trillion in assets and $580.9 billion in total net income. Also from 2002 to 2011, large partnerships—measured in terms of asset size and number of direct partners—increased significantly as well. Between those tax years, large partnerships (with 100 or more direct partners and $100 million or more in assets) increased more than 200 percent, accounting for $2.3 trillion in total assets and $69.1 billion in total net income by tax year 2011. As the size and number of these large partnerships has grown, Congress and others have raised concerns about the extent to which the Internal Revenue Service (IRS) is able to audit these entities and minimize compliance risk.

In: Large Partnerships
Editor: Francis E. Stephens
ISBN: 978-1-63463-725-1

Chapter 1

LARGE PARTNERSHIPS: WITH GROWING NUMBER OF PARTNERSHIPS, IRS NEEDS TO IMPROVE AUDIT EFFICIENCY*

United States Government Accountability Office

WHY GAO DID THIS STUDY

More businesses are organizing as partnerships while fewer are C corporations. Unlike C corporations, partnerships do not pay income taxes but pass on income and losses to their partners. Large partnerships (those GAO defined as having $100 million or more in assets and 100 or more direct and indirect partners) are growing in number and have complex structures. Some partnerships create tiers of partnerships with hundreds of thousands of partners. Tiered large partnerships are challenging for IRS to audit because tracing income through the tiers to the ultimate partners is complex.

GAO was asked to assess IRS's ability to audit large partnerships. GAO's objectives include: 1) determine what IRS knows about the number and characteristics of large partnerships, 2) assess IRS's ability to audit them, and 3) assess IRS's efforts to address the audit challenges. GAO analyzed IRS data from 2002 to 2011 and IRS audit documentation, interviewed IRS officials,

* This is an edited, reformatted and augmented version of a United States Government Accountability Office publication, No. GAO-14-732, dated September 2014.

met with IRS auditors in six focus groups, and interviewed private sector tax lawyers knowledgeable about partnerships.

What GAO Recommends

Congress should consider requiring large partnerships to identify a partner to represent them during audits and to pay taxes on audit adjustments at the partnership level. IRS should take multiple actions, including: define large partnerships, track audit results using revised audit codes, and implement project planning principles for the audit procedure projects. IRS agreed with all the recommendations, but noted that revision of the audit codes is dependent upon future funding.

What GAO Found

The number of large partnerships has more than tripled to 10,099 from tax year 2002 to 2011. Almost two-thirds of large partnerships had more than 1,000 direct and indirect partners, had six or more tiers and/or self reported being in the finance and insurance sector, with many being investment funds.

The Internal Revenue Service (IRS) audits few large partnerships. Most audits resulted in no change to the partnership's return and the aggregate change was small. Although internal control standards call for information about effective resource use, IRS has not defined what constitutes a large partnership and does not have codes to track these audits. According to IRS auditors, the audit results may be due to challenges such as finding the sources of income within multiple tiers while meeting the administrative tasks required by the Tax Equity and Fiscal Responsibility Act of 1982 (TEFRA) within specified time frames. For example, IRS auditors said that it can sometimes take months to identify the partner that represents the partnership in the audit, reducing time available to conduct the audit. TEFRA does not require large partnerships to identify this partner on tax returns. Also under TEFRA, unless the partnership elects to be taxed at the entity level (which few do), IRS must pass audit adjustments through to the ultimate partners. IRS officials stated that the process of determining each partner's share of the adjustment is paper and labor intensive. When hundreds of partners' returns have to be adjusted, the costs involved limit the number of audits IRS can conduct. Adjusting the partnership return instead of the partners' returns would reduce these costs but, without legislative action, IRS's ability to do so is limited.

IRS has initiated three projects—one of which is under development—to make large partnership audit procedures more efficient, such as identifying higher risk returns to audit. However, the two projects implemented were not developed in line with project planning principles. For example, they do not have clear and measurable goals or a method for determining results. As a consequence, IRS may not be able to tell whether the projects succeed in increasing audit efficiency.

ABBREVIATIONS

AIMS	Audit Information Management System
BRTF	Business Returns Transaction File
CDW	Compliance Data Warehouse
CMT	Compliance Management Team
ELP	Electing Large Partnership
ELPI	Enhanced Large Partnership Indicator
ERM	Enterprise Risk Management
IRC	Internal Revenue Code
IRS	Internal Revenue Service
JCT	Joint Committee on Taxation
NAICS	North American Industry Clarification System
TEFRA	Tax Equity and Fiscal Responsibility Act of 1982
TST	Tier Structure Tool
TMP	Tax Matters Partner
Treasury	U.S. Department of the Treasury

* * *

September 18, 2014

The Honorable Ron Wyden
Chairman
Committee on Finance United States Senate

The Honorable Carl Levin
Chairman

The Honorable John McCain
Ranking Member
Permanent Subcommittee on Investigations
Committee on Homeland Security and Governmental Affairs
United States Senate

In recent decades, there has been a dramatic shift in the way American businesses organize and pay taxes. The shift has been towards legal structures known as pass-through entities, such as partnerships, and away from C corporations that are subject to the corporate income tax. For example, between 2002 and 2011, the number of partnerships increased 47 percent to 3.3 million while the number of C corporations decreased by 22 percent to 1.6 million. Partnerships do not generally pay income taxes—they pass their income and losses through to their partners who report them on their income tax returns and make any associated tax payments.

Large partnerships, which we define as those with 100 or more direct and indirect partners and $100 million or more in assets, have grown even faster.[1] From 2002 to 2011, the number of large partnerships more than tripled to more than 10,000 and large partnerships hold trillions of dollars of assets.

Large partnerships create a number of tax law enforcement challenges for the Internal Revenue Service (IRS) that we have described in recent reports.[2] The challenges are due to the complexity of large partnerships as well as the number of partners. Since partnerships can be partners in other partnerships, large partnerships frequently have tiers of partnerships, creating indirect partners. Such complex structures make it difficult for IRS to find the source of income and then trace it through the tiers to the ultimate taxable partners. There are legitimate reasons for businesses to set up complex structures of entities, such as isolating one part of a business from liability for the losses of another part.

Because of the growth of large partnerships and the challenges IRS faces in auditing large partnerships, you asked us to assess IRS's ability to ensure compliance with the tax laws. Specifically, this report (1) determines what IRS knows about the number and characteristics of large partnerships; (2) determines what IRS knows about the costs and results of audits of large partnership returns and assesses IRS's ability to effectively conduct such audits; and (3) identifies and assesses IRS's efforts to address the challenges of auditing large partnership returns.

To determine the number and characteristics of large partnerships, we obtained data from IRS on tax returns filed by large partnerships for tax years

2002 to 2011.[3] Using these data, we analyzed and reported data on the number of partnerships by asset size, number of direct and indirect partners, number of tiers, and industry sector. To determine what IRS knows about the costs and results of audits of large partnership returns, we obtained audit data from IRS for fiscal years 2007 to 2013.[4] We compared the costs and results of large partnership audits to audits of corporate returns of the same asset size.[5]

To assess the effectiveness of IRS audits of large partnership returns, we reviewed relevant statutes, IRS data on large partnerships, IRS policies and procedures on partnership audits, and our recent reports on partnerships.[6] We compared information available to the intent of the partnership audit procedures outlined in statute and internal controls standards for the federal government.[7] This information included our interviews with IRS officials and private sector lawyers knowledgeable about partnerships as well as six focus groups with IRS auditors who have worked on large partnership audits. The results of the focus group data are not generalizable to all IRS audits and do not necessarily represent the official viewpoint of IRS. Instead, the results were used to identify themes in conjunction with the other forms of data we analyzed.

To identify and assess IRS's efforts to address the challenges, we reviewed IRS documents and interviewed IRS officials about the efforts. We compared information available on IRS's efforts related to large partnerships to criteria on project planning previously identified in prior GAO reports.[8] These criteria were identified by conducting a literature review of a number of guides on project management and business process reengineering.[9]

For the purposes of this review, we determined that the data used in our analysis were reliable and all dollar values have been adjusted for inflation to tax year or fiscal year 2014. Our data reliability assessment included reviewing relevant documentation, interviewing knowledgeable IRS officials, and electronic testing of the data to identify obvious errors or outliers. For additional details on our scope and methodology, see appendix I.

We conducted this performance audit from October 2013 to September 2014 in accordance with generally accepted government auditing standards. Those standards require that we plan and perform the audit to obtain sufficient, appropriate evidence to provide a reasonable basis for our findings and conclusions based on our audit objectives. We believe that the evidence obtained provides a reasonable basis for our findings and conclusions based on our audit objectives.

BACKGROUND

For tax purposes, a partnership is generally an unincorporated organization with two or more members that conducts a business and divides profits. Partnerships generally report their income on Form 1065, U.S. Return of Partnership Income. Partnerships usually do not pay income taxes but pass—or allocate—the net income or losses to partners, who pay any applicable taxes. Partnerships report the share of income or losses accruing to each partner on a Schedule K-1 with copies going to the partners and to IRS. Partners can be individuals or other entities such as corporations or other partnerships.

Forms of business organization and their tax treatment

Partnership: generally an unincorporated entity with two or more members that conducts a business, does not pay income taxes, but rather passes income or losses through to their partners, which must include that income or loss on their income tax returns.

C Corporation: a corporation that is generally taxed at the entity level under subchapter C of the Internal Revenue Code (IRC).

S Corporation: a corporation that meets certain requirements and elects to be taxed under subchapter S of the IRC, which provides that in general income and losses be passed through to its shareholders.

Source: IRS documentation. I GAO-14-732.

Having no statutory, IRS, or industry-accepted definition of a large partnership, we have defined a large partnership in two ways: 1) as having 100 or more direct and indirect partners and $100 million or more in assets, and 2) as having 100 or more direct partners and $100 million or more in assets.[10] Including just direct partners does not capture the entire size and complexity of large partnership structures. Accounting for indirect partners does, but it also raises the issue of counting income and assets more than once (described below). In this report, we generally use the definition that includes direct and indirect partners but sometimes use both definitions when the distinction might matter.

Key Terms and Examples of Partnership Structures

Partnerships can be structured as tiers of pass-through entities creating direct and indirect partners. Table 1 defines key terms for a partnership structure.

Table 1. Key Partnership Structure Terminology

Flow-through or Pass-through Entity	An entity that allocates income or losses to its taxable owners, who pay any taxes. Incometaxes generally are not paid by the pass-through entities, which include partnerships, S corporations, trusts, and estates.[a]
Taxable Partner	A partner who is the final recipient of pass-through income or loss allocations for which they owe taxes. Taxable partners include C corporations or individuals.
Direct Partner	A partner who has a direct interest in the partnership. A direct partner may be a taxable partner or a nontaxable partner.
Indirect Partner	A person holding an interest in a partnership through one or more pass-through partners.
Flow-through or Pass-through Partner	A partner which is a flow-through or pass-through entity.

Source: IRS documentation I GAO-14-732.

[a]Certain trusts are taxable trusts and do not pass through income or losses.

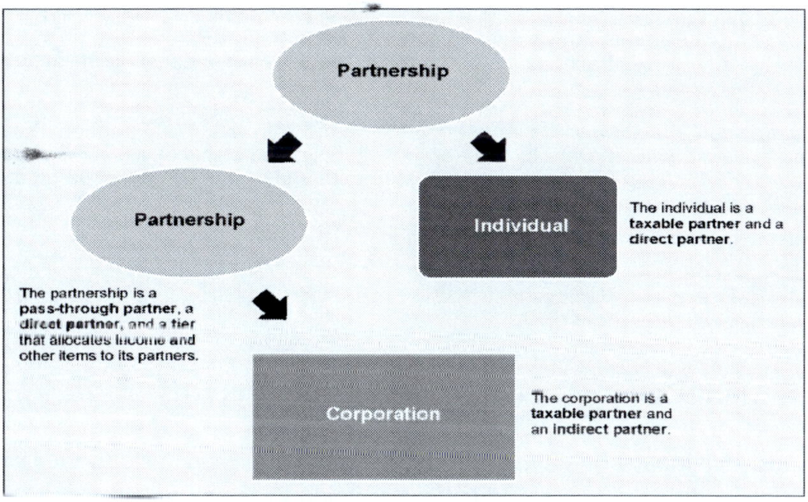

Source: GAO analysis of IRS documentation. I GAO-14-732.

Figure 1. Example of Simple Tiered Partnership Structure.

See figure 1 for an example of a simple tiered partnership structure.

For a partnership structure with multiple partners linked in networks with other partnerships, the partners, assets, and income may be counted more than once as seen in figure 2.

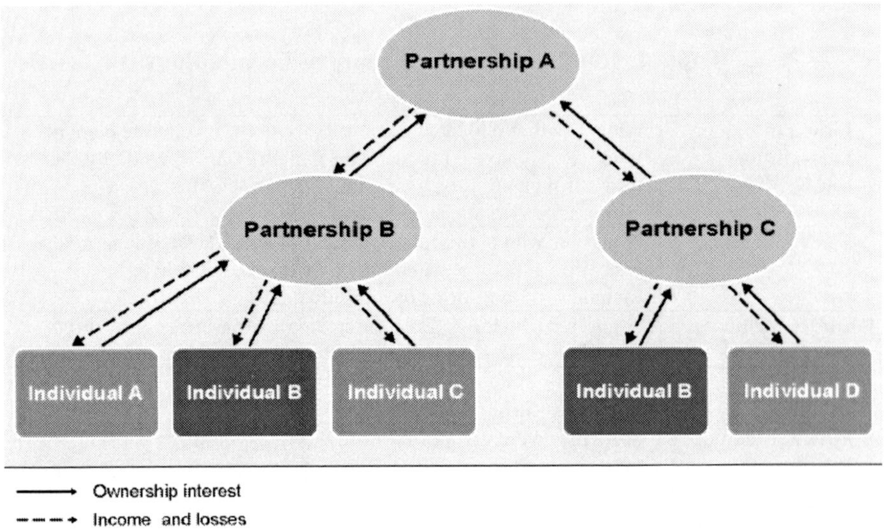

Partner, Income and Asset Counting: Partnership A has two direct partners (Partnerships B and C) and five indirect partners of which four (Individuals A-D) are unique; one of them (Individual B) is an indirect partner via both direct partners. Because income from Partnership A is divided between Partnerships B and C, adding up the total income (or assets) of all the partnerships would result in counting the income more than once.

Combining Partnerships: If a separate large partnership with 1,000 partners (Partnership D-not shown) were to buy Partnership C's ownership interest in Partnership A, then Partnership A would become a large partnership with two direct partners and 1,003 indirect partners.

Source: GAO analysis of IRS documentation. I GAO-14-732.

Figure 2. Example of Partnership Structure with Tiers and Direct and Indirect Partners.

IRS Audit Process for Large Partnership Returns

Large partnership audits typically involve two separate steps. One step is the field audit, which is a detailed examination of the partnership's tax return (Form 1065) and supporting books and records to determine whether income and losses are properly reported. The field audit may recommend adjustments to the income and losses.

The other step is called a campus audit.[11] Campus audits link partnerships to the tax returns of their direct and indirect partners. Adjustments to income or losses from the field audit may be passed through to the taxable partners responsible for paying any additional tax, based on the partners' shares in the partnership. Although IRS counts campus audits as audits, they usually do not involve an examination of a taxpayer's books and records.

Large partnership field audits follow one of two IRS procedures, which are set by statute:

Tax Equity and Fiscal Responsibility Act of 1982 (TEFRA)

In response to concerns about IRS's ability to audit partnership returns, Congress enacted specific rules regarding partnerships audits in TEFRA.[12] TEFRA audit procedures were intended to streamline IRS's partnership audit process while ensuring the rights of all partners.[13] Before TEFRA, IRS audited partners separately, leading to inconsistent treatment and making it hard to detect tax shelters.[14] According to the congressional Joint Committee on Taxation (JCT), the complexity and fragmentation of the audits—especially for large partnerships with partners in many locations—led to some audits of partners' returns ending at varying times and some partners paying additional taxes while others did not. See table 2 for key features of TEFRA.

Table 2. Select Features of Tax Equity and Fiscal Responsibility Act of 1982 (TEFRA) Audit Procedures

Consistency Reporting Requirement	Certain items, known as partnership items, are determined at the partnership level and all partners must report these items consistent with how the partnership reports them. Some items include each partner's share of the partnership's income, gain, loss, deductions, and credits.
Tax Matters Partner (TMP)	The TMP is the primary representative of the partnership in dealing with IRS as well as the partners. The TMP can be a general partner designated by the partnership or, if no TMP is designated, the general partner with largest profit interest. Under certain circumstances, IRS may select a partner to be the TMP.
Statute of Limitations	In general, a 3-year statute of limitations applies to assessments of returns of partners in TEFRA partnerships.[a]

Table 2. (Continued)

Notice and Participation Partner Rights	• Certain partners and groups are entitled to receive notices at the beginning and conclusion of the audit. • The TMP is required to keep partners informed of certain steps of the audit and the partners have the right to participate in any or all of these steps. • Certain partners can challenge IRS's findings from the audit in court, if the TMP chooses not to do so.
Timeline of Procedures	The statute and regulations define a number of timelines at stages of the audit that IRS, theTMP, or partners should complete, such as sending out the notification at the beginning and conclusion of the audit.

Source: Internal Revenue Code and IRS documentation I GAO-14-732.

[a]TEFRA also provides that the period for auditing partnerships does not expire before 3 years after the original due date of the return or date of return filing, whichever is later. This provision of TEFRA can extend, but never shorten the statute of limitations. According to IRS officials, it does audit partnerships covered by TEFRA beyond the 3-year time frame established in section 6229 in cases where the statute of limitations under section 6501 has yet to expire for one or more partners.

Ideally, once a TEFRA audit begins, it would proceed as outlined in figure 3.

Electing Large Partnership (ELP) Audit Procedures

According to the U.S. Department of Treasury (Treasury) and IRS, applying TEFRA to audits of large partnerships became an intensive and inefficient use of limited IRS resources as IRS spent more and more time on administrative tasks.[15] As a result, Congress established the Electing Large Partnerships (ELP) procedures as part of the Taxpayer Relief Act of 1997.[16] In general, the procedures apply to partnerships with 100 or more direct partners in a taxable year that elect this alternative reporting and audit framework.[17] The ELP audit procedures differ from the TEFRA procedures in two key ways: partnerships (1) may pay tax on audit adjustments instead of the partners, and (2) must report fewer items to the partners.

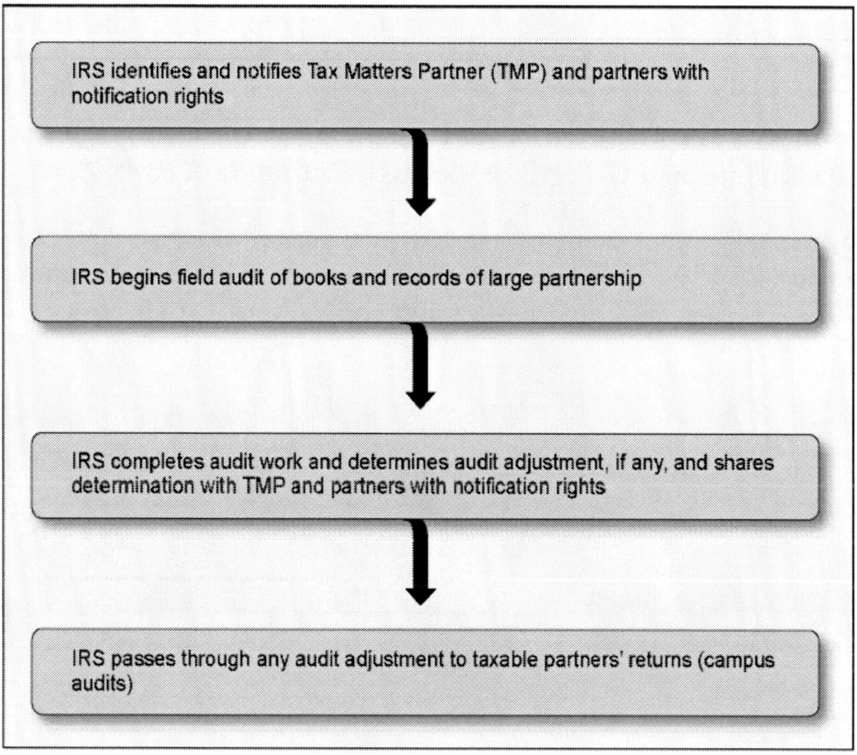

Source: GAO analysis of IRS documentation. I GAO-14-732.

Figure 3. Tax Equity and Fiscal Responsibility Act of 1982 (TEFRA) Audit Process.

IRS Resource Constraints

As we have previously reported, IRS's appropriations declined by $855 million, or 7 percent, and IRS staffing declined by more than 10,000 full-time equivalents, or 11 percent, between fiscal years 2010 and 2014.[18] Most of this staffing decline occurred in IRS enforcement, which is responsible for ensuring that tax returns, including partnership returns, comply with the tax laws.

LARGE PARTNERSHIPS HAVE GROWN IN NUMBER, SIZE, AND COMPLEXITY SINCE 2002

Businesses Have Shifted From Organizing as C Corporations to Partnerships and Other Pass-through Entities in Recent Years

During tax years 2002 through 2011, the number of partnerships and S corporations of all sizes increased 47 percent and 32 percent, respectively, while the number of C corporations decreased 22 percent.[19] See figure 4.

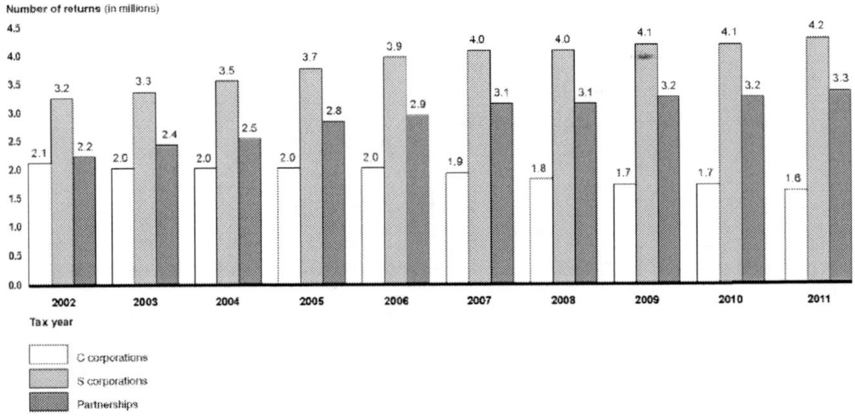

Source: GAO analysis of IRS data. I GAO-14-732.

Note: C Corporations are generally taxed at the entity level under subchapter C of the Internal Revenue Code (IRC) whereas S corporations are corporations that meet certain requirements and elect to be taxed under subchapter S of the IRC, which provides that income and losses usually pass through to their shareholders.

Figure 4. Number of Returns by Form of Business, Tax Years 2002 to 2011.

The Number of Large Partnerships Has More Than Tripled

During tax years 2002 through 2011, the number of large partnerships with 100 or more direct and indirect partners as well as $100 million or more in assets more than tripled to 10,099—an increase of 257 percent. Over the same years, total assets of these large partnerships (without accounting for double counting) increased 289 percent to almost $7.5 trillion.[20] Figure 5 shows the increase in the number of large partnerships for various asset sizes.

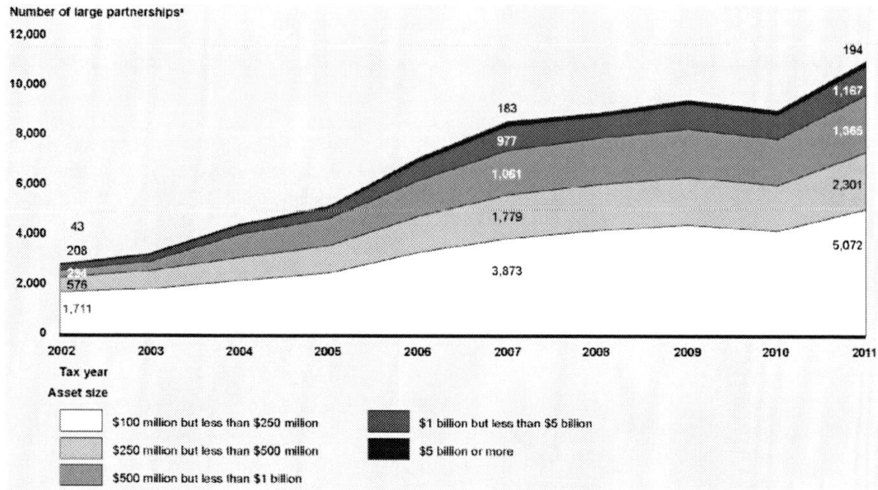

Source: GAO analysis of IRS data from Enhanced Large Partnership Indicator File and Business Returns Transaction File, Compliance Data Warehouse. I GAO-14-732.

[a]Some large partnerships may not have reached the $100 million asset threshold without ownership interests in other partnerships. The average asset size is also higher than it would be without those ownership interests. IRS data do not indicate how many large partnerships would have fallen below the $100 million threshold without their ownership interests in other partnerships.

Figure 5. Large Partnerships, Defined to Include Direct and Indirect Partners, by Asset Size, Tax Years 2002 to 2011.

Most Large Partnerships Have Complex Structures with Thousands of Partners and Multiple Tiers

Almost two-thirds of large partnerships had 1,000 or more direct and indirect partners in tax year 2011, but hundreds of large partnerships had more than 100,000 partners. Large partnerships with the most direct and indirect partners had the greatest increase from tax years 2002 to 2011. See figure 6.

The number of large partnerships varies considerably from year to year due in part to investment choices made by other large partnerships. One IRS official said that the partnerships with more than a million partners increased from 17 in tax year 2011 to 1,809 in tax year 2012. The official attributed most of the increase to a small number of investment funds that expanded their interests in other partnerships. If those investment funds choose to divest their interests in other partnerships, the number of large partnerships would decrease significantly.

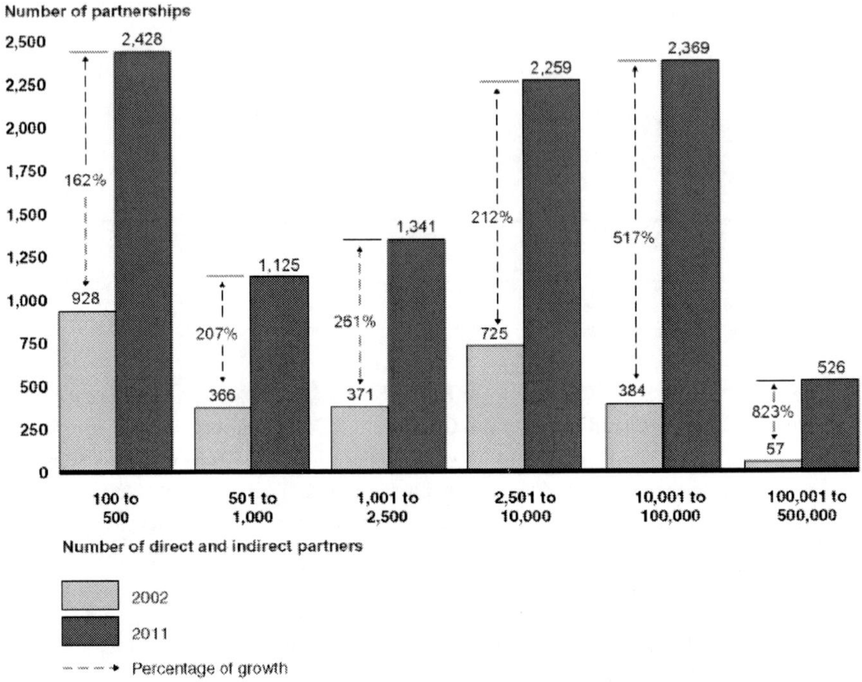

Source: GAO analysis of IRS data from Enhanced Large Partnership Indicator File and Business Returns Transaction File, Compliance Data Warehouse. I GAO-14-732.

Note: Although 51 large partnerships had 500,000 or more direct and indirect partners in tax year 2011, we did not show the percent increase to avoid disclosure of information about specific taxpayers as the 2002 value is less than 10. Assuming a value of 10 in tax year 2002, this group of large partnerships increased 410 percent by tax year 2011. The growth rate would be higher if the value in 2002 was less than 10.

Figure 6. Number of and Percentage Increase in Large Partnerships, by Direct and Indirect Partners, Tax Years 2002 and 2011.

Tiering contributes to complexity. In tax year 2011, more than two-thirds of large partnerships had at least 100 or more pass-through entities and 36 percent had at least 1,000 or more pass-through entities as direct and indirect partners. These pass-through entities may be direct partners or may exist at various tiers below the direct partners. There is some evidence that large partnership structures are becoming more complex. In tax year 2011, 78 percent of the large partnerships had six or more tiers compared to 66 percent in tax year 2002.[21]

Tiering complicates determining the relationships and allocations of income and losses within a large partnership structure. For example, in figure 7, the allocation from the audited partnership on the far left side of the figure passes through eight partnerships along the bolded path before it reaches one of its ultimate owners on the right. This path also may not be the only path from the audited partnership to the ultimate owner.

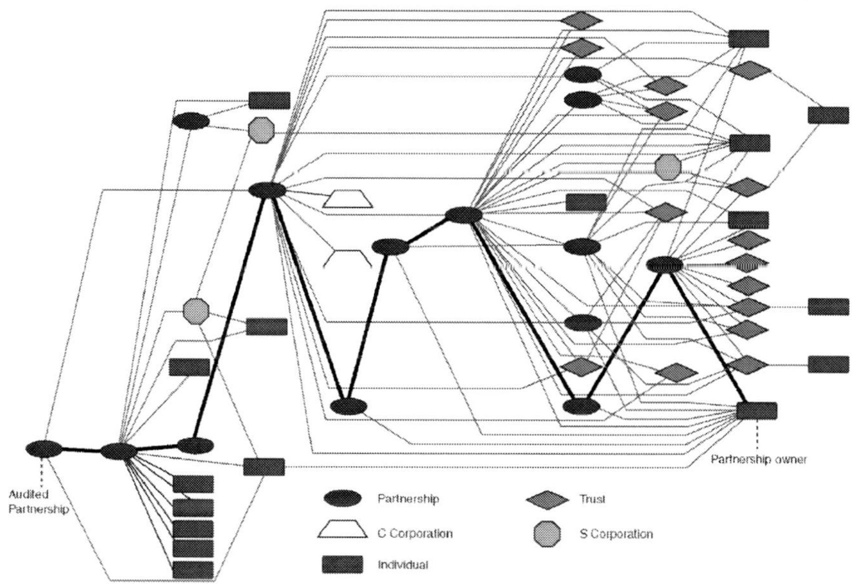

Source: GAO analysis of IRS documentation. I GAO-14-732.

Note: This figure, adapted from IRS documentation, illustrates a hypothetical, complex partnership structure, which shows the relationship between various types of entities. The allocation of income and losses from the audited partnership on the far left side crosses eight pass-through entities, all of which are partnerships, along the bolded line before it reaches one of its ultimate partnership owners on the right side. This figure was originally used in our report on business networks. See *Tax Gap: IRS Can Improve Efforts to Address Tax Evasion by Networks of Businesses and Related Entities*, GAO-10-968 (Washington, D.C.: Sept. 24, 2010).

Figure 7. Example of Partnership Structure.

While this example of a partnership structure is complex, it has only 50 partners and 10 tiers. Large partnership structures could be much more complex. In 2011, 17 large partnerships had more than a million partners.

According to an IRS official, several large partnerships have more than 50 tiers.

Large Partnerships Are Concentrated in the Finance Sector

In tax year 2011, about 73 percent of large partnerships reported being in the finance and insurance sector, up from 64 percent in tax year 2002 (see table 3).[22] About 87 percent of those in the finance and insurance sector in tax year 2011 engaged in financial investment activities, of which about 70 percent reported $1 billion or more in assets.

Table 3. Number and Percentage of Large Partnerships by Industry Group (Self Reported), Tax Year 2002 and 2011

	Tax Year			
	Number		Percentage	
	2002	2011	2002	2011
Mining	18	170	1%	2%
Manufacturing	23	142	1%	1%
Transportation and Warehousing	43	114	2%	1%
Finance and Insurance	1,799	7,333	64%	73%
Real Estate, Rental, and Leasing	695	1,507	25%	15%
Professional, Scientific, and Technical Services	55	129	2%	1%
Holding Companies	56	233	2%	2%
Other	143	471	5%	5%

Source: GAO analysis of IRS data from Enhanced Large Partnership Indicator File and Business Returns Transaction File, Compliance Data Warehouse. I GAO-14-732.

Note: Industry classifications are based on the North American Industry Classification System (NAICS). NAICS codes are self reported by businesses and judgment may be needed to determine the most appropriate NAICS code.

As we previously found, many of the large partnerships in the finance and insurance sector are investment funds, such as hedge funds and private equity funds, which are pools of assets shared by investors.[23] See appendix II for additional data on the number and characteristics of large partnerships.

IRS Audits Few Large Partnerships due to Challenges Presented by the Complexity of Both the Partnership Structures and Audit Procedures

IRS Audits Less Than 1 Percent of Large Partnerships

IRS audits few large, complex partnerships. According to IRS data, in fiscal year 2012, IRS closed 84 field audits—or a 0.8 percent audit rate.[24] This audit rate is well below that of C corporations with $100 million or more in assets, which was 27.1 percent in fiscal year 2012. See table 4.

Table 4. Audit Rate for Large Partnerships and Large Corporations, Fiscal Years 2007 to 2013

	Fiscal Year						
	2007	2008	2009	2010	2011	2012	2013
Large Partnerships							
Audit Rate	0.5%	0.6	0.6	1.4	0.7	0.8	N/A
Large Corporations							
Audit Rate	20.6	21.4	20.8	20.6	23.1	27.1	27.4

Source: GAO analysis of IRS data from IRS data book and Audit Information Management System, Compliance Data Warehouse. I GAO-14-732.

Note: For any large partnership, the number of audited returns closed in a fiscal year may include returns from multiple tax years. Calendar year 2012 partnership filings were not available when we did our analysis to compute the audit rate for fiscal year 2013.

This audit rate does not depend on whether large partnerships are defined to include direct and indirect partners or only direct partners. Our interim report, which focused on only direct partners in defining large partnerships, also showed a 0.8 percent audit rate in 2012.[25]

It is possible that some large partnership audits in table 4 are audits of different partnerships within the same large partnership structure. For example, if IRS audits one large partnership and then discovers that it needs to audit another large partnership in the same complex structure, those would count as two separate audits. Available IRS data did not allow us to determine how often this occurred.

Audits of Large Partnerships Resulted in Minimal Changes to Partnership Returns

Table 5 shows that most large partnership field audits closed from fiscal years 2007 through 2013 did not find tax noncompliance. In 2013, for example, 64.2 percent of the large partnership audits resulted in no change to the reported income or losses. In comparison, IRS audits of C corporations with $100 million or more in assets had much lower no change rates, as also shown in table 5. In addition, IRS audits of all partnerships, not just large partnerships, also had a lower no change rate of 47 percent in fiscal year 2013.

Table 5. No Change Rate for Large Partnerships and Large Corporations, Fiscal Years 2007 to 2013

	Fiscal Year						
	2007	2008	2009	2010	2011	2012	2013
Large Partnerships							
No Change Rate	85.3	77.8	82.6	51.6	77.0	66.7	64.2
Large Corporations							
No Change Rate	16.2	22.1	18.6	18.7	20.4	27.2	21.4

Source: GAO analysis of IRS data from IRS data book and Audit Information Management System, Compliance Data Warehouse. I GAO-14-732.

Note: For partnerships, the no change rate means that the audits made no changes to the partnership's reported income, loss, deductions, or credits reflected on the tax return or Schedule(s) K-1 for partners, which are information returns that the partnership sends to the partners to report partners' share of the partnership's income, deductions, credits, etc. The no change rate for corporations means that the audits made no changes in the tax liability reported on the corporate tax return (e.g., tax, penalties, or refundable credits).

According to IRS focus group participants, large partnership returns have the potential for a high tax noncompliance risk. However, it is not clear whether the high no change rate for large partnership audits is due to IRS selecting large partnerships that were tax compliant or is due to an inability of IRS audits to identify noncompliance, as discussed below.

When field audits of large partnerships resulted in changes, the aggregate amount was minimal, as shown in table 6.[26] This could be because positive changes on some audits were cancelled out by negative changes on other audits. In 3 of the 7 years shown in table 6, the total adjustments from the field audits were negative; that is, they favored the large partnerships being audited. This did not occur for audits of large corporations.

Table 6. Total and Average Recommended Audit Adjustments to Net Income for Large Partnership and to Additional Taxes for Large Corporate for Field Audits, Fiscal Years 2007 to 2013 (dollars in millions)

	Fiscal Year						
	2007	2008	2009	2010	2011	2012	2013
Large Partnerships (Adjustments to income)							
Total	$ (99.2)	(46.4)	22.5	75.7	569.5	160.4	(370.4)
Average	(2.9)	(1.0)	0.5	0.6	9.3	1.9	(3.9)
Large Corporations (Adjustments to tax liability)							
Total	21,967	22,595	26,864	22,824	22,984	15,952	14,895
Average	5.2	5.0	5.6	5.1	4.7	2.8	2.4

Source: GAO analysis of IRS data from IRS data book and Audit Information Management System, Compliance Data Warehouse. I GAO-14-732.

IRS data show that its large partnership audits used fewer resources than large corporate audits, but still required significant audit staff time, as shown in table 7.

Table 7. Audit Time Measures for Field Audits of Large Partnership and Large Corporations, Fiscal Years 2007 to 2013

	Fiscal Year						
	2007	2008	2009	2010	2011	2012	2013
Large Partnerships							
Average field hours charged	139	383	164	104	255	255	409
Average calendar days spent on field audits	467	382	381	307	341	513	555
Large Corporations							
Average field hours charged	791	724	694	694	580	521	496
Average calendar days spent on field audits	709	658	601	585	556	536	598

Source: GAO analysis of IRS data from IRS data from Audit Information Management System, Compliance Data Warehouse. I GAO-14-732.

These field audit time measures for large partnerships do not cover all audit costs, such as the time spent passing through audit adjustments at the campus. For example, if the campus passes through audit adjustments to 100 partners of one large partnership (which means opening 100 campus audits), the total cost of the related large partnership audit may be significantly larger than the field audit time accounted for partnerships in table 7. However, the campus does not track the total hours spent working all the partners' returns related to a partnership return audited in the field due to limitations associated with IRS information systems, which are discussed below. Campus officials noted that working returns related to large partnerships require significant time and resources given their growing complexity and size.

IRS Reporting of Partnership Audit Data Does Not Provide Clear Picture of Large Partnership Audits

IRS data that report audit results for partnerships do not break out large partnerships, which would help inform audit resource allocation decisions. Without such a break out, our analysis of audit data for large partnerships relied on combining various databases. According to standards for internal control in the federal government, managers need accurate and complete information to help ensure efficient and effective use of resources.[27] IRS officials acknowledged that they need a better understanding of large partnership audits to improve resource allocation.

The problem arises because IRS's audit data codes—known as activity codes—are not specific enough to identify large partnerships. 28 IRS uses its activity codes to set goals for the number of returns IRS plans to audit in a fiscal year and track audit results. Because they do not identify large partnership returns, the current activity codes do not allow IRS to do the kind of analysis needed to plan resource usage, including the level of audit and support staff needed, for large partnership audits.

IRS has developed new activity codes that would distinguish partnership returns based on asset size and the type of income reported; but they are not scheduled to begin reporting the new activity codes until fiscal year 2017 due to resource limitations. IRS has not decided which activity codes would be used to define large partnership returns. Further, the new activity codes do not account for the number of partners, which IRS has identified as a major driver of resource usage for large partnership audits—particularly for the work done at the campus. If these IRS activity codes do not account for such a driver of resource usage, IRS will not be able to make effective resource allocation decisions.

Revising the activity codes requires defining a large partnership for audit purposes, which IRS has not done. The exact definition matters less than ensuring that one definition is consistently applied so that there is agreement on the scope of large partnership audit efforts and results can be assessed.

IRS also does not distinguish between field audits and campus audits in counting the number of large partnership audits. When calculating its audit rate for all partnerships, IRS accounts for both field audits and campus audits, which misrepresents the number of audits that actually verify information reported on tax returns. Unless IRS separately accounts for field and campus audits, it cannot accurately measure audit results.

Several Challenges Related to Complexity May Limit IRS's Ability to Audit Large Partnerships and to Recommend Changes

IRS officials said that they do not have sufficient data on the results from field audits of large partnerships to know what is driving the high no change rate and minimal tax changes.[29] Our focus groups with IRS field auditors and interviews with IRS officials, however, provided insights on the challenges to finding noncompliance in field audits.

Complex Large Partnership Structures Make Audits and Detecting Noncompliance Challenging

The complexities arising from large partnership structures challenge IRS's ability to identify tax noncompliance. For example, IRS officials reported having difficulty identifying the business purpose for the large partnerships or knowing which entity in a tiered structure is generating the income or losses. In these cases, IRS auditors said they do not know with which partner or tier of the partnership structure to start the audit. Without finding the source of income and losses, it is difficult for IRS to determine whether a tax shelter exists, an abusive tax transaction is being used, or if income and losses are being properly characterized. Focus group participants said that complex structures could mask tax noncompliance. For example, one participant said

> I think noncompliance of large partnerships is high because a lot of what we have seen in terms of complexity and tiers of partnership structures... I don't see what the driver is to create large partnership structures other than for tax purposes to make it difficult to identify income sources and tax shelters.

Source: IRS focus group participant. I GAO-14-732.

IRS officials stated that determining compliance is especially challenging when auditing the returns of hedge funds that often have an interest in many other partnerships and in investments—such as financial derivatives that are complex and constantly changing, and can involve noncompliance, as we have previously found.[30] Focus group participants noted that the complexity requires them to invest extensive time to research and understand the structure of large partnerships and technical tax issues. For example, one focus group participant noted the difficulty of auditing the returns of large, complex partnerships:

> ... [Because] income is pushed down so many tiers, you are never able to find out where the real problems or duplication of deductions exist. The reporting of income, expenses could be duplicated but there is no way to figure it out unless you drill down and audit all tiers, all tax returns.

Source: IRS focus group participant. I GAO-14-732.

TEFRA Audit Procedures Add Complexity to Audits of Large Partnerships

As the number and complexity of large partnerships have increased, aspects of the TEFRA audit procedures have become an impediment, according to focus groups and interviews with IRS officials.

TEFRA Reduces Time IRS Can Actually Spend on Audits

IRS focus group participants stated that the interaction of TEFRA procedures with increasingly complex partnership structures has reduced the amount of time to effectively audit the return within the statute of limitations. A 3-year statute of limitations governs the time in which IRS must complete its audits of partnerships, which begins on the due date of the return or date of return filing, whichever is later. IRS on average takes about 18 months after a large partnership return is received until the audit is started, leaving another 18 months to actually conduct an audit, as illustrated in figure 8. After the field audit, TEFRA generally requires that any audit adjustments be passed through to partners within a 1-year assessment period.

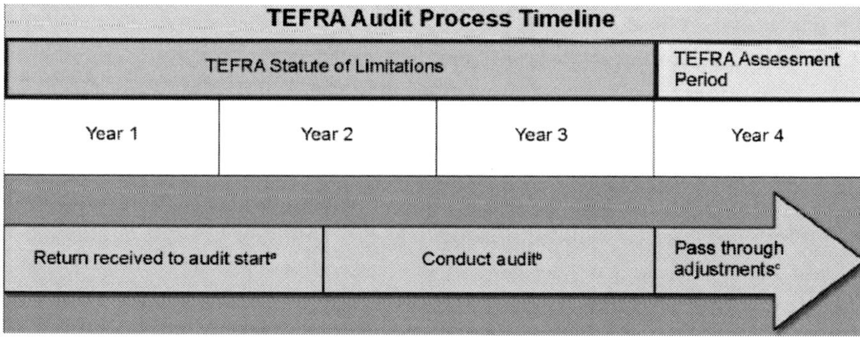

Source: GAO analysis of IRS data and documentation. I GAO-14-732.

Notes: A 3-year statute of limitations governs the time to complete partnership audits.

[a]In fiscal year 2013, IRS took an average of 1.4 years from when a large partnership return is received to start the audit.

[b]In fiscal year 2013, IRS took an average of 1.5 years to conduct a large partnership audit.

[c]IRS generally completes within 1-year the assessment of audit adjustments to partners of the large partnership.

Figure 8. Tax Equity and Fiscal Responsibility Act of 1982 (TEFRA) Audit Timeline.

Focus group participants said that they sometimes run out of time on the statute of limitations and have to close the audit as no change.[31] IRS has no data that supports this claim as it does not break out audit results by large partnerships, as discussed earlier.

Identifying the Tax Matters Partner (TMP) Can Take Months

TEFRA defines the responsibilities of the TMP, such as providing information to IRS as well as communicating with partners, which generally help to facilitate the audit. Without a TMP, IRS is not able to conduct the audit. Further, if the audit proceeds without a qualified TMP, the partners may challenge any settlement agreed to between the IRS and the unqualified TMP at the conclusion of the audit, so IRS takes steps to ensure that any TMP is a qualified TMP.[32]

IRS focus group participants said that identifying a qualified TMP is a primary challenge in large partnership audits. The burden of doing so falls largely on IRS, taking time and effort away from doing the actual audit work. For example, TEFRA does not require partnerships to designate a TMP on their returns. In addition, TEFRA allows the TMP to be an entity, not a person. In either case, IRS auditors spend time requesting that the partnership designate a TMP or tracking down an actual person to act as a representative for the TMP—unless the partnership chose to list that person on the Form 1065. IRS focus group participants cited various reasons for not being able to immediately identify the TMP. Some said that large partnerships are purposely unclear about the TMP as an audit-delay strategy. As one participant said:

> Entities will often be elusive about designating the Tax Matters Partner. The entities will use this tactic as a first line of defense against an audit.

Source: IRS focus group participant. I GAO-14-732.

If a large partnership does not designate a TMP on the partnership return, IRS will provide the partnership the opportunity to do so. If the partnership does not, TEFRA requires that the partner with the largest profit interest automatically becomes the TMP. However, if IRS determines that it is impracticable to apply this rule, then IRS may designate the TMP.[33] IRS officials said that they are hesitant to do so before giving the partnership an opportunity to designate a TMP because the IRS designation may be opposed by the partners and IRS needs to collect information to find a partner that meets the criteria. As a consequence, exercising this authority can still mean that the start of audit is delayed. However, if IRS were to move directly to the largest profit interest rule or chose to designate the TMP using its existing authority instead of reaching out to the partnership, IRS could save valuable time during the average 18-month window it has to completes the audit. IRS does not track data on the time spent identifying the TMP. Focus group participants said that identifying and qualifying the designated TMP could take weeks or months. Losing a few months from the 18 months to audit a large partnership could be significant to IRS field auditors.

IRS officials said IRS has issued new job aids and training on identifying the TMP, clarified TMP requirements, and added a section about TEFRA in the December 2013 revision of IRS Publication 541, *Partnerships*. However, these steps do not solve the fundamental problem of limited audit time being lost while identifying a TMP. A legislative change to TEFRA requiring all large partnerships to designate a TMP on their tax returns and to provide updated TMP information to IRS once an audit starts would solve the problem. Without such a change, IRS's field audits of large partnerships are inefficient which hinders its ability to fulfill its mission of ensuring tax law compliance. The costs of such a legislative change should be low. There would be no increased costs to IRS—the change would reduce IRS's costs. Partnerships already have partners responsible for filing tax returns so designating a TMP should not be onerous.

IRS Has Difficulty Utilizing the 45-Day Rule Due to Complexity of Large Partnerships

Another TEFRA audit procedure that is meant to benefit IRS but is difficult to use is the TEFRA 45-day rule.[34] IRS's TEFRA regulations allow IRS to withdraw its notification to the TMP about the start of the audit, within 45 days of notifying the TMP. If IRS does so within 45 days, IRS can close the audit as no change without having to notify the partners.[35]

IRS focus group participants said that they often do not have sufficient information to determine whether to close an audit within 45 days. In addition, time spent identifying the TMP reduces the time available to make this determination. As a result, of the 61 field audits of large partnerships closed in fiscal year 2013 as no change, none were closed within the 45-day period.[36] IRS has the authority under TEFRA to amend its regulation to lengthen this period for withdrawing an audit notice beyond 45 days without having to notify all the partners of the withdrawal. Extending the notice withdrawal period would save IRS audit resources and allow the resources to be more effectively used in ensuring tax law compliance.

Passing Through Audit Adjustments to Numerous Partners May Not be Worth the Effort

TEFRA generally requires that audit adjustments be passed through to the taxable partners. Although IRS does not track the costs for the campus to pass field audit adjustments through to the partners, campus officials said the costs are high for a number of reasons.

- The process of linking partnership returns (Forms 1065), Schedule K-1s, and partners' returns (Forms 1040) is largely manual and paper driven. According to IRS officials, the campus information systems do not have the capability to automate the process. Paper copies of all these returns must be retrieved and linked in a very labor intensive process.
- The portion of the partnership audit adjustment that gets passed through to each partner must be manually determined by using the ownership share reported on the relevant Schedule K-1.
- The Schedule K-1 information may not always be accurate, as we have previously found, requiring IRS to contact the partnership and

review the partnership agreement to clarify ownership shares among the partners.[37]

- A copy of the partnership agreement must usually be requested from the partnership being audited and for potentially each partnership within the partnership structure that is linked. Partnership agreements may include special allocation for some income items that supersede the ownership interest reported on the Schedule K-1.[38] Finding special allocations requires detailed reviews of the partnership agreements of the partnerships within the partnership structure. According to IRS officials, this step cannot be automated. IRS officials also said that partnerships could provide special allocation schedules to IRS, which would eliminate the need to review the entire agreement.

As a consequence, the process for passing audit adjustments through to partners is costly and very time consuming. This limits the number of large partnerships that IRS can audit. Furthermore, since IRS generally has one year after the 3-year statute of limitations ends to pass through adjustments, the campus has to start linking returns before it knows whether there will be an audit adjustment or whether an adjustment will be large enough to merit passing through. In a large partnership, dividing the adjustment among hundreds or thousands of partners may result in amounts that are so small that IRS deems them not worth the cost to pass through. IRS officials said that they do not track how often the audit adjustments are not passed through and how much unpaid tax is not collected as a result. IRS campus officials estimated that they close 50,000 to 60,000 returns for all partnerships each year and further estimated that 65 to 70 percent of these are closed without passing through any adjustment.

IRS is unable to track aggregate campus audit costs and campus adjustments associated with a field audit due to limitations of its information systems. IRS has requested funding in its fiscal year 2014 and 2015 budget proposals for an updated information system that would allow it to automate the linking process and collect more robust data but funding has not been approved.

Large Partnerships May Pay Tax on Audit Adjustments Rather Than Pass Them Through to the Partners but Such Payments are Not Widely Used

Current law allows large partnerships to pay a tax owed as determined by audit adjustments at the entity level rather than passing the adjustments through to partners, which would avoid all the costs of campus audits. This is allowed under both the Electing Large Partnership (ELP) audit procedures and under IRS procedures for closing audits with what is called a closing agreement. However, few large partnerships elect to become an ELP.[39] Further, partnerships must voluntarily agree to use a closing agreement to pay a tax at the entity level and few do so.

The Chairman of the House of Representatives Committee on Ways and Means and the Administration have also put forth proposals to address some of the challenges of auditing large partnerships. 40 While the proposals differ somewhat and apply to partnerships with different numbers of partners, both would allow IRS to collect tax at the partnership level instead of having to pass it through to the taxable partners. For example, the Administration developed a legislative proposal to make the ELP audit procedures mandatory for partnerships with 1,000 or more direct and indirect partners, known as the Required Large Partnership proposal. IRS officials said that these legislative proposals, if passed, would significantly help address challenges involved with passing through audit adjustments. These proposals would involve tradeoffs and decisions about how to treat partners. For example, because the partners may be taxed at different tax rates, the single tax rate applied to the net audit adjustment at the partnership level may be different than the rate partners would pay if the adjustment was passed through.

IRS Field Auditors Face Barriers Accessing Timely Support and Training to Address Complexities

IRS focus group participants stated that they do not have the needed level of timely support from IRS counsel, TEFRA coordinators, and specialists. Focus group participants said that the support is critical because they had limited knowledge of the technical tax issues for partnerships and they may only work on a partnership audit once every few years. Further, focus group participants stated that it can take weeks or months to get needed input and planning audits is difficult because they do not know how long it will take to get the needed stakeholder input. Unexpected delays reduce the average18-month window of time for audit work. Focus group participants said that some IRS locations have only one TEFRA coordinator to answer questions about partnership audits. For example, IRS has one TEFRA coordinator to support all audits in New York State. IRS officials said that the number of TEFRA coordinators declined from 28 in fiscal year 2006 to 20 in May 2014 while workload increased. One IRS official said that TEFRA coordinators have to respond to requests for assistance and review and process TEFRA audits for partnerships of all sizes, not only large partnerships. IRS officials said that they plan to hire two coordinators in fiscal year 2014 and five in fiscal year 2015.[41]

IRS counsel officials told us that they believe that the number of delayed responses is fairly low, in contrast to what focus group participants said, and IRS counsel strives to process all requests for legal advice within 45 days of receipt. However, IRS counsel officials said that they do not track the number of requests for large partnership audits; if known, the response time would help IRS auditors to plan their audit work. Such a change would be in line with IRS's strategic plan, which has a strategic objective on utilizing data to make timely, informed decisions.[42] In addition to help from stakeholders, IRS focus groups participants told us that they have trouble accessing refresher courses on TEFRA and partnership tax issues. IRS officials told us that IRS field auditors may not understand that such training is available and can be taken with the permission of their supervisors. They also said that such training is not usually mandatory and some auditors may choose to not take it. Ensuring IRS auditors have access to training would be in line with IRS's current strategic plan, which highlights the importance of building a talented workforce. IRS officials stated that they are developing and have implemented new tools and training to assist auditors with TEFRA rules and procedures. However, IRS's Large Business and International division—the division responsible for auditing large partnership returns— experienced a 92 percent reduction in available training funds from 2009 to 2013. [43] IRS officials said that this reduction meant eliminating face-to-face training and relying on new virtual training courses on TEFRA and partnership audits in general.

IRS Has Initiated Efforts That May Address Some Large Partnership Audit Challenges but Their Potential to Have Significant Impact Is Unclear

IRS has limited ability to directly address some of the challenges it faces auditing large partnerships. For example, IRS cannot make tiered partnerships less complex nor change the TEFRA audit procedures that are set in statute. Nevertheless, IRS has initiated three projects to improve its large partnership audit procedures. IRS has also begun an effort to better manage enterprise risk.

Audit Procedures Improvement Projects Are Missing Some Planning and Evaluation Steps

Table 8 describes the three audit procedure projects and their potential for addressing certain challenges based on our interviews with IRS officials and reviews of available limited documents.

Table 8. IRS Efforts and Their Potential to Address Some Challenges in Auditing Large Partnership Returns

Efforts	Potential to Address Challenges
Large Partnership Compliance Management Team (CMT) pilot—test process to identify noncompliance by partnerships with 1,000 or more direct or indirect partners	• Help fieldaudits team better understand large partnership structure and potential noncompliance issues. • Improve selection of partner returns to link and management of pass-throughprocess. • Provide support to field audit teams through pass-through specialists.
Large Partnership Procedures—use audit tools and new procedures for audits of partnerships with at least 100 direct or indirect partners[a]	• Make field audit teams aware of large partnership returns. • Assess the noncompliance on returns to review before the audits start.
Just-In-Time Linkage pilot—test ways to better manage the linkage workload and process at the campus	• Analyze the structure of the large partnership when its return is selected for audit and a linkage request is submitted to the campus. • Wait to link partner returns until the field team has a better idea of the audit adjustment. • Seek information on special allocations when a linkage request for a partnership return selected for audit is submitted to the campus.

Source: GAO interviews of IRS officials and review of IRS documents. I GAO-14-732.

[a] The tools include yK-1, which allows examiners to obtain a visual representation of the partnership structure, and the Tier Structure Tool (TST), which uses the yK-1 database to generate reports on the investment structure of any pass-through entity Procedures include: (1) using TST to identify large partnership returns); (2) marking these returns with an large partnership indicator; (3) notifying IRS staff about returns with noncompliance; (4) delivering instructions for using audit tools to assess noncompliance; and (5) assembling information gathered for use during audits.

The two field audit-related projects (the Large Partnership CMT and Large Partnership Procedures) started in 2013. IRS officials said that it could be a few years before enough audits are completed to know whether the two efforts worked as intended. The project to improve the campus linkage process (Just-In-Time Linkage pilot) started August 2014, but it is still under development and IRS provided limited documentation detailing the development of this effort.

IRS has not developed the two field audit-related projects consistent with project planning principles, as shown in table 9.[44] These two projects did not meet three of the five principles.

Table 9. Assessment of IRS's Field Audit-Related Projects for Large Partnerships

Project Planning Principles	Large Partnership Efforts	
	Large Partnership Compliance Management Team	Large Partnership Procedures
Develop a project plan with clear and measurable goals, schedules, and resources	Did not develop a project plan.	Did not develop a project plan.
Evaluate human resources by assessing how needed resources will be acquired and retained	Identified resource and expertise needs.	Evaluated resource gaps in the audit process and ensured resources available for new procedures.
Leverage stakeholder input and incorporate lessons learned by evaluating past performance	Involved relevant stakeholders.	Involved relevant stakeholders.
Analyze and mitigate risks by evaluating, prioritizing, and documenting risks as well as options for mitigating risks.	Did not sufficiently evaluate mitigation options or contingency plans.	Did not sufficiently evaluate mitigation options or contingency plans.
Monitor progress by collecting data to determine effectiveness in achieving the stated goals	Did not clearly show how data collected would be used to monitor progress.	Did not develop a mechanism for collectingdata to monitor progress.

Source: GAO-12-696, GAO-04-37, GAO analysis of IRS documentation, and GAO interviews of IRS officials. I GAO-14-732.

For the Large Partnership CMT, while IRS officials said that they plan to collect data on five metrics, it is unclear how the metrics will be used to monitor progress because they are not specific to the CMT.[45] Without following the principles in table 9, IRS may not be able to assess whether the projects succeeded in making large partnership audits more efficient and effective.

IRS Has Not Determined How Large Partnerships Should Be Incorporated Into Its Enterprise-Wide Risk Management

IRS began an enterprise risk management (ERM) program agency wide in 2014. According to IRS documentation, IRS needed to evaluate how risks are identified, prioritized, evaluated, and mitigated across the agency. ERM objectives include deploying resources effectively, identifying and managing cross-enterprise risks, identifying the level of risk IRS is willing to absorb, aligning that risk level with strategies, and reducing operational surprises, among others.

Large partnership audits and the challenges associated with them raise a number of the issues listed as ERM objectives. Because of the lack of information IRS currently collects and tracks about large partnership audits, it does not have a very clear picture of how effectively its audit resources are being utilized. Nevertheless, as large partnerships grow in number, IRS will have to make decisions about whether to reallocate audit resources away from other compliance work to conduct more large partnership audits.

IRS has not yet determined how large partnerships will be incorporated into its ERM effort. Without such a determination and without documentation of the risks considered, IRS managers and external stakeholders, including Congress, may lack a record of how compliance risks associated with large partnerships were identified and prioritized. We have previously reported on the benefits of risk management and identified elements of a risk-management framework.[46] Risk management is a strategy for helping program managers and stakeholders make decisions about assessing risk, allocating resources, and taking actions under conditions of uncertainty. We recognize that IRS's information systems currently provide little data on large partnerships, as noted in other sections of this report. Even though IRS is not explicitly planning for how many large partnerships to audit each year, it is devoting resources to such audits. IRS is implicitly making decisions about how to allocate audit resources between large partnerships and other types of taxpayers. A determination about how large partnership compliance risks are to be identified and weighed against the compliance risks of other types of taxpayers would better inform those decisions.

CONCLUSION

Large partnerships are a significant part of the economy and are increasing in number, size, and complexity. However, the relatively low rate at which IRS audits large partnerships and the minimal results achieved raise concerns about IRS's ability to ensure the tax compliance of large partnerships. IRS has little data available to know why its audits are finding so little tax noncompliance. That is because IRS has not consistently defined "large partnership"—accounting for both the number of partners and amount of assets—and devised a related coding system to track any audit results. Without such data, IRS cannot conduct analysis to identify ways to better plan and use IRS resources in auditing large partnerships as well as analyze whether large partnerships present a high noncompliance risk.

Without the data, testimonial evidence from IRS auditors indicates that they feel challenged to audit complicated partnerships for compliance without sufficient time and support. Existing audit procedures set in law and in IRS regulations add to the time pressures and constrain IRS auditors. Because so little is currently known about large partnership noncompliance, it would be premature to try to design overall, long-term solutions. An incremental approach could be based on what is currently known, including legislative changes that Congress should consider as well as actions that IRS should take.

Legislative changes could help IRS auditors deal with the time constraints and reduce the resource demands of large partnership audits. Requiring large partnerships to designate a qualified TMP that the field auditors can contact is a relatively simple step that could reduce audit delays. Requiring large partnerships to pay any tax due at the entity level would also save resources but would not be a simple change. Such a change would have differing impacts on partners who may be in different tax brackets. The change would save the resources that are now devoted to the paper driven, labor intensive process of passing adjustments through to large numbers of partners. Paying taxes due on audit adjustments at the entity level has advantages over other options for audit efficiency gains such as automating the current paper driven process. Even if IRS was given resources to modernize its campus information systems, parts of the adjustment pass-through process would continue to require labor intensive reviews of partnership agreements.

IRS can take several actions that would begin to provide better information about large partnership compliance and audit results, or that could lower audit costs. Actions that would be a first step towards better information for analyzing large partnership compliance include developing a consistent definition of a large partnership along with activity codes that could be used to track audit results. To lower audit costs and avoid wasting audit staff time, IRS could change its practice governing when to use its authority to select a TMP, and the regulation which established the number of days an audit can be open without triggering more costly closing procedures. IRS could also better ensure that limited calendar time is not wasted in an audit. It could do so by tracking delays in providing expert support, clarify when auditors can expect such support, and then use this information about the support that can realistically be provided to better plan the number and scope of new audits, so that the time allowed under the statute of limitations is more effectively used.

While IRS has initiated three projects to improve its audit procedures, it has not followed project planning principles, including taking the steps needed to effectively track the results for the two projects that have been implemented. Without doing so, IRS will not know whether the projects succeeded in improving audit procedures.

As large partnerships continue to grow in number and complexity, IRS will have to make strategic decisions about whether to reallocate scarce audit resources from other categories of taxpayers—perhaps from C corporations which are declining in number—to conduct more large partnership audits. IRS's new Enterprise Risk Management program provides a venue for weighing the compliance risks associated with large partnerships against those of other types of taxpayers.

MATTERS FOR CONGRESSIONAL CONSIDERATION

Congress should consider altering the TEFRA audit procedures to:

- Require partnerships that have more than a certain number of direct and indirect partners to pay any tax owed as determined by audit adjustments at the partnership level.

- Require partnerships to designate a qualified TMP and, if that TMP is an entity, to also identify a representative who is an individual and for partnerships to keep the designation up to date.

RECOMMENDATIONS FOR EXECUTIVE ACTION

We recommend that the Commissioner of Internal Revenue take the following eight actions:

- Track the results of large partnerships audits: (a) define a large partnership based on asset size and number of partners; (b) revise the activity codes to align with the large partnership definition; and (c) separately account for field audits and campus audits.
- Analyze the audit results by these activity codes and types of audits to identify opportunities to better plan and use IRS resources in auditing large partnerships.
- Use existing authority to promptly designate the TMP under the largest profits interest rule or some other criterion.
- Extend the 45-day rule to give field audit teams more flexibility on when to withdraw an audit notice.
- Help field auditors for large partnership audits receive the support they request from counsel staff, TEFRA coordinators, and IRS specialists: (a) track the number of requests and time taken to respond; (b) clarify when responses to their requests should be expected; and (c) use the tracked and clarified information when planning the number and scope of large partnership audits.
- Clarify how and when field auditors can access refresher training on TEFRA audit procedures and partnership tax law.
- Develop and implement large partnership efforts in line with the five leading principles for project planning and track the results to identify whether the efforts worked as intended.
- Make and document a determination about how large partnerships are to be incorporated into the Enterprise Risk Management process.

Agency Comments and Our Evaluation

We provided a draft of this report for review and comment to the Commissioner of Internal Revenue. We received written comments dated September 8, 2014 from IRS's Deputy Commissioner for Services and Enforcement. We also received technical comments from IRS, which we incorporated into the final report where appropriate.

In its written comments, IRS agreed with our recommendations but said two of our recommendations, related to revising IRS's activity codes to enable tracking large partnership audits and then analyzing audit results, are dependent upon future funding. We acknowledge in the report the resource constraints IRS currently faces. However, continuing to audit large partnerships with limited ability to track and analyze audit results will not help IRS make sound resource allocation decisions or improve audit effectiveness.

James R. White
Director, Tax Issues Strategic Issues

Appendix I: Objectives, Scope, and Methodology

The objectives of this report are to (1) determine what IRS knows about the number and characteristics of large partnerships; (2) determine what IRS knows about the costs and results of audits of large partnership returns and assess IRS's ability to effectively conduct such audits; and (3) identify and assess IRS's efforts to address the challenges of auditing large partnership returns.

To determine the number and characteristics of large partnerships, we obtained data on tax returns filed by large partnerships from the Enhanced Large Partnership Indicator (ELPI) file on partnerships for tax years 2002 to 2011, and on the number of partnerships with 100 or more direct and indirect partners and $100 million or more in assets. We merged these data with data obtained from the Business Returns Transaction File (BRTF). We analyzed and reported ELPI and BRTF data by the total number of partnerships by asset size, direct partner size, indirect partner size, industry group, and tiering depth. The ELPI data file captures information about the ownership structure of large partnerships. The ELPI file starts with a partnership and traces Schedule K-1 allocations through to the ultimate taxpayer. ELPI traces the ownership structure of a partnership as long as either the depth is less than 11 tiers or the ownership percentage is greater than 0.00001 percent and therefore can present a picture of the approximate number of direct and indirect partners in a partnership structure. The ELPI currently only has data on partnerships that file a 1065 and not those that file a 1065-B. For similar analysis on partnerships that file a 1065-B, see our prior work on large partnerships.[1]

To determine the number of IRS audits of large partnership returns and the characteristics of those audits, we obtained data from the Audit Information Management System (AIMS) and reported those partnership returns subject to IRS audit that were closed during fiscal years 2007 to 2013.[2] Once we identified the audited population of large partnership returns, we only reported those audits that were traditional IRS field audits (in which IRS audited the books and records of a large partnership return), and not campus audits (in which IRS usually passed audit adjustments through to the related partners' returns), as they are mainly an administrative function and do not include an examination of the books and records of the taxpayer return in question. We analyzed the results from these data consistent with how IRS measures audit results, such as the audit coverage rate (partnership returns subject to audit as a percentage of the total partnership return population) and no change rate (those audits that resulted in no change to the tax return from the audit), and, where possible, without suppressing data due to disclosure requirements, by asset size. We also analyzed the hours and days spent on large partnership audits to assess the costs of these audits. Where data were available, we compared these measures for large partnership return audits to those for corporate return audits of the same asset size.

To assess the effectiveness of IRS audits of large partnership returns, we interviewed officials in the Office of Chief Counsel, Large Business and International division, Small Business and Self-Employed division, and Research, Analysis, and Statistics division. We also interviewed a number of external private sector lawyers who are knowledgeable about partnership tax law, reviewed academic research and literature, reviewed IRS documentation, such as IRS policies and procedures on partnership audits, and reviewed our recent reports on partnerships.[3] We also completed six focus groups with 30 IRS team coordinators and managers on the challenges associated with completing audits of large partnership returns. These team coordinators and managers were selected for our focus groups because they supervised or worked on a large partnership return audit, based on our definition of large partnerships above, which was closed in calendar year 2013. Where available, we supplemented the challenges identified in these focus groups with supporting data and documentation to provide context or support those challenges identified. We performed a content analysis on the six focus groups, using NVivo software, to analyze and categorize the themes of the focus groups.[4] The results of the focus group data are not generalizable to all IRS audits and do not necessarily represent the official viewpoint of IRS. Instead the results are used to identify themes in conjunction with the other data we collected. We compared information available to the intent of the partnership audit procedures outlined in statute.[5] In addition, we compared information available on audits of large partnership returns to *Standards for Internal Control in the Federal Government* (GAO/AIMD-00-21.3.1, November 1999).[6] To identify and assess IRS efforts to address the challenges of audits of large partnership returns, we reviewed IRS documentation and interviewed IRS officials to identify any efforts and initiatives they have ongoing related to large partnership. We assessed IRS's efforts and initiatives related to large partnerships using project planning criteria that our prior work identified work as leading practices.[7] We identified these criteria by conducting a literature review of a number of guides on project management and business process reengineering.[8]

For the purposes of this review, we determined that the data used in our analysis were sufficiently reliable for our purposes and all dollar values have been adjusted for inflation to tax year or fiscal year 2014. Our data reliability assessment included reviewing relevant documentation, conducting interviews with knowledgeable IRS officials, and conducting electronic testing of the data to identify obvious errors or outliers. All Statistics of Income estimates in this report have 95 percent confidence intervals that are within +/- 10 percent of the point estimate, unless otherwise specified. Based on IRS documents and interviews with IRS officials, data in the ELPI file may be incomplete since this file is based on Schedule K-1 data. For example, some Schedule K-1s may be missing from the database because partnerships did not file Schedule K-1s, IRS errors, and timing problems. In general, the depth of tiering in ELPI for a partnership structure represents a minimum amount resulting in approximate entity counts because the missing data would add more entities that qualify for our definition of large partnerships. We conducted this performance audit from October 2013 to September 2014 in accordance with generally accepted government auditing standards. Those standards require that we plan and perform the audit to obtain sufficient, appropriate evidence to provide a reasonable basis for our findings and conclusions based on our audit objectives. We believe that the evidence obtained provides a reasonable basis for our findings and conclusions based on our audit objectives.

APPENDIX II: ADDITIONAL DATA ON NUMBER AND CHARACTERISTICS OF LARGE PARTNERSHIPS

Table 10. Large Partnerships by Average and Median Number of Direct Partners, and Direct and Indirect Partners, Tax Years 2002 to 2011

	Tax Year									
	2002	2003	2004	2005	2006	2007	2008	2009	2010	2011
Average and Median Number of Direct Partners										
Average	453	531	595	622	585	587	631	899	934	980
Median	38	42	43	43	32	32	25	27	28	26
Average and Median Number of Direct and Indirect Partners										
Average	12,007	8,150	9,346	16,882	30,674	73,684	61,269	113,722	14,721	29,998
Median	1,352	1,327	1,549	1,414	1,757	1,793	3,133	3,071	1,619	2,776

Source: GAO analysis of IRS data from the Enhanced Large Partnership Indicator (ELPI) File and Business Returns Transaction File, Compliance Data Warehouse. I GAO-14-732.

Note: Because the ELPI file does not have complete K-1 data from Schedule(s) K-1 for partners, which are information returns that the partnership sends to the partners to report partners' share of the partnership's income, deductions, credits, etc., the extent of tiering represents a minimum amount and entity counts are approximate.

Table 11. Large Partnerships by Number of Direct and Indirect Partners, Tax Years 2002 to 2011

	Tax Year									
	2002	2003	2004	2005	2006	2007	2008	2009	2010	2011
Number of Direct and Indirect Partners										
100 to 500	928	1,086	1,228	1,471	1,825	2,114	1,941	2,060	2,505	2,428
501 to 1,000	366	371	519	549	787	1,007	873	934	1,013	1,125
1,001 to 2,500	371	513	478	731	1,032	1,255	982	1,075	1,288	1,341
2,501 to 10,000	725	852	1,118	1,189	1,645	1,766	1,135	1,476	1,931	2,259
10,001 to 100,000	384	352	533	578	1,025	744	1,928	1,224	1,339	2,369
100,001 to 500,000	57	68	65	d	d	85	1,146	743	113	526
501,000 or more	d	0	d	76	198	902	79	1,088	70	51

Legend: d = Value not shown to avoid disclosure of information about specific taxpayers.

Source: GAO analysis of IRS data from the Enhanced Large Partnership Indicator (ELPI) File and Business Returns Transaction File, Compliance Data Warehouse. I GAO-14-732.

Note: Because the ELPI file does not have complete K-1 data from Schedule(s) K-1 for partners, which are information returns that the partnership sends to the partners to report partners' share of the partnership's income, deductions, credits, etc., the extent of tiering represents a minimum amount and entity counts are approximate.

Table 12. Large Partnerships by Number of Direct Partners, Tax Years 2002 to 2011

	Tax Year									
	2002	2003	2004	2005	2006	2007	2008	2009	2010	2011
Number of Direct Partners										
0 to 99	2,149	2,401	2,920	3,376	4,934	5,949	6,193	6,618	6,487	7,892
100 to 500	558	680	837	1,003	1,302	1,600	1,592	1,673	1,476	1,869
501 to 1,000	30	40	51	59	82	110	100	85	82	109
1,001 to 2,500	34	40	44	53	58	56	52	56	50	48
2,501 to 10,000	37	48	52	67	79	74	69	57	51	61
10,001 to 100,000	23	32	43	41	58	79	68	94	96	97
100,001 to 500,000	d	d	d	d	d	d	d	17	17	21
501,000 or more	0	0	0	0	0	0	0	0	0	d

Legend: d = Value not shown to avoid disclosure of information about specific taxpayers.

Source: GAO analysis of IRS data from the Enhanced Large Partnership Indicator (ELPI) File and Business Returns Transaction File, Compliance Data Warehouse. I GAO-14-732.

Note: Because the ELPI file does not have complete K-1 data from Schedule(s) K-1 for partners, which are information returns that the partnership sends to the partners to report partners' share of the partnership's income, deductions, credits, etc., the extent of tiering represents a minimum amount and entity counts are approximate.

Table 13. Average Asset Size of Large Partnerships and Number of Large Partnerships by Asset Size, Tax Years 2002 to 2011 (dollars in millions)

	Tax Year									
	2002	2003	2004	2005	2006	2007	2008	2009	2010	2011
Average Asset Size	$ 680	$ 698	$ 771	$ 728	$ 889	$ 911	$ 754	$ 764	$ 794	$ 741
Asset Size	Number of Partnerships									
$100 million but less than $250 million	1,711	1,834	2,174	2,480	3,315	3,873	4,210	4,426	4,190	5,072
$250 million but less than $500 million	576	732	924	1,094	1,448	1,779	1,855	1,934	1,851	2,301
$500 million but less than $1 billion	294	360	454	532	855	1,061	1,013	1,078	1,076	1,365
$1 billion but less than $5 billion	208	266	341	424	744	977	869	1,002	975	1,167
$5 billion or more	43	50	56	72	156	183	137	160	167	194

Source: GAO analysis of IRS data from the Enhanced Large Partnership Indicator (ELPI) File and Business Returns Transaction File, Compliance Data Warehouse. I GAO-14-732.

Notes: Some of the large partnerships may not have reached the $100 million asset threshold without their ownership interests in other partnerships. The average asset size is also higher than it would be without those ownership interests. IRS data doesn't allow us to determine how many large partnerships would have fallen below the $100 million threshold without their ownership interests in other partnerships. Because the ELPI file does not have complete K-1 data from Schedule(s) K-1 for partners, which are information returns that the partnership sends to the partners to report partners' share of the partnership's income, deductions, credits, etc., the extent of tiering represents a minimum amount and entity counts are approximate.

Table 14. Average Tier Depth of Large Partnerships and Number of Large Partnerships by Tier Depth, Tax Years 2002 to 2011

	Tax Year									
	2002	2003	2004	2005	2006	2007	2008	2009	2010	2011
Average Tier Depth	7	7	7	7	8	8	8	8	8	8
Tier Depth	Number of Partnerships									
1 tier	35	44	47	50	59	62	61	55	59	62
2 tiers	68	85	91	95	107	148	144	142	137	155
3 to 5 tiers	871	957	1,131	1,345	1,619	1,836	1,744	1,743	2,019	1,967
6 to 10 tiers	1,013	1,502	1,832	2,191	3,053	3,422	2,999	2,894	3,596	3,542
11 or more tiers	845	654	848	921	1,680	2,405	3,136	3,766	2,448	4,373

Source: GAO analysis of IRS data from the Enhanced Large Partnership Indicator (ELPI) File and Business Returns Transaction File, Compliance Data Warehouse. I GAO-14-732.

Note: Because the ELPI file does not have complete K-1 data from Schedule(s) K-1 for partners, which are information returns that the partnership sends to the partners to report partners' share of the partnership's income, deductions, credits, etc., the extent of tiering represents a minimum amount and entity counts are approximate.

Table 15. Average Number of Pass-through Partners and Large Partnerships by Number of Pass-through Partners, Tax Years 2002 to 2011

	Tax Year									
	2002	2003	2004	2005	2006	2007	2008	2009	2010	2011
Average Number of Pass-Through Partners	1,090	901	1,012	1,614	2,753	5,544	5,203	9,506	1,583	3,420
Number of Pass-Through Partners	Number of Partnerships									
Zero	35	44	46	50	58	61	61	53	55	59
1 to 100 pass-through partners	1,131	1,285	1,516	1,768	2,254	2,681	2,401	2,568	3,039	2,868
101 to 1,000 pass-through partners	1,140	1,374	1,649	1,899	2,649	3,114	2,992	2,634	3,211	3,496
1,001 to 2,500 pass-through partners	326	302	428	501	808	787	1,045	880	994	1,365
2,501-10,000 pass-through partners	148	174	228	298	539	251	353	740	777	1,488
10,001-50,000 pass-through partners	52	63	82	d	17	949	1,190	784	143	775
50,001 or more pass-through partners	0	0	0	76	193	30	42	941	40	48

Legend: d = Value not shown to avoid disclosure of information about specific taxpayers.

Source: GAO analysis of IRS data from the Enhanced Large Partnership Indicator (ELPI) File and Business Returns Transaction File, Compliance Data Warehouse. I GAO-14-732.

Note: Because the ELPI file does not have complete K-1 data from Schedule(s) K-1 for partners, which are information returns that the partnership sends to the partners to report partners' share of the partnership's income, deductions, credits, etc., the extent of tiering represents a minimum amount and entity counts are approximate.

Table 16. Number of Large Partnerships by Industry Group, Tax Years 2002 to 2011

	Tax Year									
Industry Group	2002	2003	2004	2005	2006	2007	2008	2009	2010	2011
Mining	18	32	35	44	76	99	131	129	127	170
Manufacturing	23	25	27	39	56	85	105	108	116	142
Transportation and Warehousing	43	43	51	40	56	61	92	87	96	114
Finance and Insurance	1,799	2,195	2,715	3,190	4,731	5,707	5,530	6,124	5,955	7,333
Real Estate, Rental, and Leasing	695	685	782	870	1,081	1,275	1,486	1,401	1,287	1,507
Professional, Scientific, and Technical Services	55	57	69	74	85	86	108	109	98	129
Holding Companies	56	53	72	89	113	157	186	200	193	233
Other	143	152	198	256	320	403	446	442	387	471

Source: GAO analysis of IRS data from the Enhanced Large Partnership Indicator (ELPI) File and Business Returns Transaction File, Compliance Data Warehouse. I GAO-14-732.

Notes: Industry classifications are based on the North American Industry Classification System (NAICS). NAICS codes are self reported by businesses and judgment may be needed to determine the most appropriate industry code. Because the ELPI file does not have complete K-1 data, which is based on Schedule(s) K-1 for partners, which are information returns that the partnership sends to the partners to report partners' share of the partnership's income, deductions, credits, etc, the extent of tiering represents a minimum amount and entity counts are approximate.

APPENDIX III: DATA ON AUDITS OF LARGE PARTNERSHIPS AND LARGE CORPORATE RETURNS

Table 17. Number of Field Audits of Large Partnership Returns and Field Audit Coverage Rate by Asset Size, Fiscal Years 2007 to 2013

	Fiscal year						
Asset Size	2007	2008	2009	2010	2011	2012	2013[a]
	Number of Field Audits						
$100 million or more	**34**	**45**	**46**	**122**	**61**	**84**	**95**
	Field Audit Coverage Rate						
$100 million or more	**0.5%**	**0.6**	**0.6**	**1.4**	**0.7**	**0.8**	**N/A**
$100 million but less than $250 million	**0.4**	**0.5**	**0.4**	**1.0**	**0.5**	**0.7**	**N/A**
$250 million but less than $1 billion	**0.6**	**0.6**	**0.7**	**1.7**	**0.9**	**0.5**	**N/A**
$1 billion or more	**d**	**d**	**d**	**2.2**	**1.4**	**2.0**	**N/A**

Legend: d = Value not shown to avoid disclosure of information about specific taxpayers.

Source: GAO analysis of IRS data from Audit Information Management System, Compliance Data Warehouse. I GAO-14-732.

Notes: The audit coverage rate calculations are determined by dividing those partnership returns that were audited in the current fiscal year by those returns filed in the previous calendar year. The number of audits closed in a given fiscal year may include multiple returns of the same taxpayer from different tax years that were closed in the same fiscal year. The number of returns filed in the previous calendar year would not be adjusted in this case.

[a]Calendar year 2012 partnership filings were not available at the time we completed our analysis to determine the audit coverage rate for fiscal year 2013.

Table 18. Field Audit No Change Rate for Audits of Large Partnership Returns by Asset Size, Fiscal Years 2007 to 2013

	Fiscal year						
Asset Size	2007	2008	2009	2010	2011	2012	2013
$100 million or more	**85.3%**	**77.8**	**82.6**	**51.6**	**77.0**	**66.7**	**64.2**
$100 million but less than $250 million	**85.7**	**94.4**	**100.0**	**52.3**	**85.0**	**58.3**	**69.2**
$250 million but less than $1 billion	**92.3**	**d**	**75.0**	**50.0**	**68.0**	**65.0**	**76.5**
$1 billion or more	**d**	**d**	**d**	**53.8**	**81.3**	**78.6**	**48.6**

Legend: d = Value not shown to avoid disclosure of information about specific taxpayers.

Source: GAO analysis of IRS data from Audit Information Management System, Compliance Data Warehouse. I GAO-14-732.

Notes: For entities, such as partnerships that pass through income or losses to the partners of the business, the no change results from these audits meant that there were no changes made to the entities' reported income, loss, deductions, or credits reflected on the tax return or Schedule(s) K-1 for partners of the partnership.

Table 19. Number of Field Audits of Corporate Returns By Asset Size, Fiscal Years 2007 to 2013

	Fiscal Year						
Asset Size	2007	2008	2009	2010	2011	2012	2013
$100 million or more	**4,212**	**4,556**	**4,781**	**4,471**	**4,855**	**5,784**	**6,150**
$100 million but less than $250 million	**904**	**1,006**	**1,106**	**1,166**	**1,271**	**1,800**	**1,540**
$250 million but less than $500 million	**580**	**635**	**749**	**735**	**778**	**1,043**	**1,025**
$500 million but less than $1 billion	**573**	**606**	**658**	**581**	**663**	**774**	**937**
$1 billion but less than $5 billion	**1,116**	**1,197**	**1,167**	**1,060**	**1,160**	**1,217**	**1,554**
$5 billion but less than $20 billion	**596**	**652**	**593**	**498**	**562**	**535**	**711**
$20 billion or more	**443**	**460**	**508**	**431**	**421**	**415**	**383**

Source: GAO analysis of IRS data from IRS data book. I GAO-14-732.

Note: For the highest two asset brackets for fiscal year 2012, we combine correspondence audits (audits completed by mail) and field audits as the IRS Data Book does not report the number of field audits separately to avoid disclosure of information about specific taxpayers.

Table 20. Field Audit Coverage Rate of Corporate Returns, By Asset Size, Fiscal Years 2007 to 2013

	Fiscal year						
Asset Size	2007	2008	2009	2010	2011	2012[a]	2013
$100 million or more	**20.6%**	**21.4**	**20.8**	**20.6**	**23.1**	**27.1**	**27.4**
$100 million but less than $250 million	**11.5**	12.6	13.3	14.4	16.4	22.5	18.8
$250 million but less than $500 million	13.1	13.8	15.5	15.7	17.0	22.1	21.4
$500 million but less than $1 billion	18.1	18.1	17.7	17.1	20.1	22.1	26.4
$1 billion but less than $5 billion	30.6	30.3	26.4	26.9	30.2	30.0	36.4
$5 billion but less than $20 billion	61.8	61.7	47.2	43.7	49.8	45.4	57.2
$20 billion or more	118.4	124.7	112.6	96.4	93.6	93.0	86.3

Source: GAO analysis of IRS data from IRS data book. I GAO-14-732.

Notes: Audit coverage rate is calculated in the IRS data book are determined by dividing the number of audits of corporate returns completed in the current fiscal year by the number of returns filed in the prior calendar year. The percentage of returns audited may be greater than 100 percent of the returns filed in the previous calendar year since audits may be conducted in one fiscal year on returns filed in multiple prior calendar years.

[a]For the audit coverage rate calculation for fiscal year 2012, we combine correspondence audits (audits completed by mail) and field audits in the calculations for the highest two asset brackets as the IRS Data Book does not report the number of field audits separately to avoid disclosure of information about specific taxpayers.

Table 21. No Change Rates for Field Audits of Corporate Returns by Asset Size, Fiscal Years 2007 to 2013

	Fiscal Year						
Asset Size	2007	2008	2009	2010	2011	2012	2013
$100 million or more	**16.2%**	**22.1**	**18.6**	**18.7**	**20.4**	**27.2**	**21.4**
$100 million but less than $250 million	**24**	**26**	**31**	**32**	**29**	**33**	**32**
$250 million but less than $500 million	**20**	**22**	**27**	**24**	**28**	**27**	**24**
$500 million but less than $1 billion	**20**	**20**	**16**	**20**	**24**	**24**	**21**
$1 billion but less than $5 billion	**13**	**14**	**15**	**12**	**15**	**16**	**16**
$5 billion but less than $20 billion	**10**	**6**	**8**	**6**	**9**	**8**	**15**
$20 billion or more	**7**	**4**	**3**	**3**	**5**	**4**	**7**

Source: GAO analysis of IRS data from IRS data book. I GAO-14-732.

Notes: The no change rate includes corporate returns audited in which there were no changes in tax liability (e.g., tax, penalties, or refundable credits).

Table 22. Total Audit Adjustment for Field Audits of Corporate Returns By Asset Size, Fiscal Years 2007 to 2013 (dollars in millions)

	Fiscal Year						
Asset Size	2007	2008	2009	2010	2011	2012	2013
$100 million or more	**$ 21,967**	**22,595**	**26,824**	**22,824**	**22,984**	**15,952**	**14,895**
$100 million but less than $250 million	**284**	**319**	**378**	**609**	**239**	**224**	**302**
$250 million but less than $500 million	**597**	**208**	**584**	**300**	**155**	**356**	**188**
$500 million but less than $1 billion	**376**	**517**	**897**	**597**	**258**	**223**	**228**
$1 billion but less than $5 billion	**3,514**	**2,858**	**3,619**	**2,606**	**2,611**	**2,510**	**2,244**
$5 billion but less than $20 billion	**4,555**	**5,714**	**7,779**	**6,149**	**6,178**	**2,963**	**3,442**
$20 billion or more	**12,641**	**12,980**	**13,608**	**12,563**	**13,543**	**9,675**	**8,491**

Source: GAO analysis of IRS data from *IRS Data Book*. I GAO-14-732.

Note: The total recommended additional tax for fiscal year 2012 for the $100 million or more, $5 billion but less than $20 billion, and $20 billion or more asset brackets includes the total recommended additional tax from both correspondence audits (audits completed by mail) and field audits because the field audit amounts were not disclosed in the IRS Data Book for those asset brackets to avoid disclosure of information about specific taxpayers.

Table 23. Average Audit Adjustment for Field Audits of Corporate Returns By Asset Size, Fiscal Years 2007 to 2013 (dollars in millions)

	Fiscal Year						
Asset Size	2007	2008	2009	2010	2011	2012	2013
$100 million or more	**$ 5.2**	**5.0**	**5.6**	**5.1**	**4.7**	**2.8**	**2.4**
$100 million but less than $250 million	**0.3**	**0.3**	**0.3**	**0.5**	**0.2**	**0.1**	**0.2**
$250 million but less than $500 million	**1.0**	**0.3**	**0.8**	**0.4**	**0.2**	**0.3**	**0.2**
$500 million but less than $1 billion	**0.7**	**0.9**	**1.4**	**1.0**	**0.4**	**0.3**	**0.2**
$1 billion but less than $5 billion	**3.1**	**2.4**	**3.1**	**2.5**	**2.3**	**2.1**	**1.4**
$5 billion but less than $20 billion	**7.6**	**8.8**	**13.1**	**12.3**	**11.0**	**5.5**	**4.8**
$20 billion or more	**28.5**	**28.2**	**26.8**	**29.1**	**32.2**	**23.3**	**22.2**

Source: GAO analysis of IRS data from *IRS Data Book*. I GAO-14-732.

Note: The average recommended additional tax per corporate return audit for fiscal year 2012 for the $100 million or more, $5 billion but less than $20 billion, and $20 billion or more asset brackets includes the average recommended additional tax per corporate return from both correspondence audits (audits completed by mail) and field audits because the field audit amounts were not disclosed in the IRS Data Book for those asset brackets to avoid disclosure of information about specific taxpayers.

Table 24. Average IRS Hours Charged on Audits of Large Corporate Returns By Asset Size, Fiscal Years 2007 to 2013

	Fiscal Year						
Asset Size	2007	2008	2009	2010	2011	2012	2013
$100 million or more	791	724	694	694	580	521	496
$100 million but less than $250 million	226	235	233	203	172	185	213
$250 million but less than $500 million	263	280	295	270	190	216	203
$500 million but less than $1 billion	381	376	398	342	286	285	278
$1 billion but less than $5 billion	714	672	622	646	551	498	448
$5 billion but less than $20 billion	1,430	1,164	1,181	1,147	1,187	1,186	911
$20 billion or more	2,600	2,371	2,271	2,844	2,272	2,468	2,334

Source: GAO analysis of IRS data from *IRS Data Book* and Audit Information Management System, Centralized Information System. I GAO-14-732.

Table 25. Average Number of Calendar Days That Audits of Large Corporate Returns Were Open at IRS By Asset Size, Fiscal Years 2007 to 2013

	Fiscal Year						
Asset Size	2007	2008	2009	2010	2011	2012	2013
$100 million or more	709	658	601	585	556	536	598
$100 million but less than $250 million	465	440	374	370	364	374	458
$250 million but less than $500 million	517	461	444	451	409	408	486
$500 million but less than $1 billion	600	524	559	564	493	545	576
$1 billion but less than $5 billion	800	731	654	663	617	661	639
$5 billion but less than $20 billion	942	866	781	814	803	731	793
$20 billion or more	1,091	1,095	1,048	965	1,008	937	974

Source: GAO analysis of IRS data from *IRS Data Book* and Audit Information Management System, Centralized Information System. I GAO-14-732.

Table 26. Average Number of Calendar Days from Return Processing to IRS Audit Closure for Large Corporate Returns By Asset Size, Fiscal Years 2007 to 2013

	Fiscal Year						
Asset Size	2007	2008	2009	2010	2011	2012	2013
$100 million or more	1,306	1,132	1,064	1,003	1,092	1,095	1,181
$100 million but less than $250 million	1,050	855	789	759	898	931	1,027
$250 million but less than $500 million	1,101	909	853	889	1,020	1,015	1,085
$500 million but less than $1 billion	1,195	975	1,047	1,026	992	1,171	1,212
$1 billion but less than $5 billion	1,358	1,225	1,135	1,089	1,139	1,255	1,237
$5 billion but less than $20 billion	1,643	1,324	1,338	1,246	1,389	1,235	1,357
$20 billion or more	1,691	1,732	1,509	1,319	1,436	1,222	1,416

Source: GAO analysis of IRS data from *IRS Data Book* and Audit Information Management System, Centralized Information System. I GAO-14-732.

End Notes

[1] Direct partners are partners that have a direct interest in the large partnership during the tax year. Direct partners may include taxable partners (such as a corporation or individual) and nontaxable partners (such as a partnership) that also have direct partners. Indirect partners are partners that have an interest in a partnership through interest in another partnership or other form of pass-through entity.

[2] Our recent report and testimony on large partnerships highlighted their growth and the challenges IRS faces in auditing these entities. See GAO, *Large Partnerships: Characteristics of Population and IRS Audits,* GAO-14-379R (Washington, D.C.: Mar. 19, 2014) and *Large Partnerships: Growing Population and Complexity Hinder Effective IRS Audits,* GAO-14-746T (Washington, D.C.: July 22, 2014). For details about all partnerships, see GAO, *Partnerships and S Corporations: IRS Needs to Improve Information to Address Tax Noncompliance,* GAO-14-453 (Washington, D.C.: May 14, 2014).

[3] For this report, we only report data on those partnerships that filed a Form 1065, U.S. Return of Partnership Income, because the database we used to identify large partnerships, the Enhanced Large Partnership Indicator (ELPI) file, does not capture data on large partnerships that filed a 1065-B, U.S. Return of Income for Electing Large Partnerships. For more information see GAO-14-379R.

[4] IRS does not have a category in its audit data for "large partnerships." To identify the population of large partnership returns that IRS audited, we first identified the number of large partnerships that filed a return and then merged that population with IRS's audit data. Because we focused on large partnership returns filed from tax year 2002 through 2011, returns filed prior to 2002 and then audited by IRS during fiscal years 2007 to 2013 would not be included in the data we report. We report information on a fiscal year basis because IRS reports its tax enforcement information by fiscal year in its annual data book. See IRS *Data Book 2013*, Publication 55B (Washington, D.C.: March 2014). The fiscal year that the audit closes usually accounts for audit work done in that year as well as prior years.

[5] Data cover partnerships that filed Form 1065, U.S. Return of Partnership Income, and had 100 or more direct and indirect partners and $100 million or more in assets. Data on the number and characteristics of partnerships are from the Enhanced Large Partnership Indicator and Business Return Transaction File while audit data are from the Audit Information Management System.

[6] See GAO-14-379R, GAO-14-746T, and GAO-14-453.

[7] Pub. L. No. 97-248, §§ 401–407, 96 Stat. 324, 648–671 (1982), Joint Committee on Taxation, *General Explanation of the Revenue Provisions of the Tax Equity and Fiscal Responsibility Act of 1982*, JCS-38-82 (Washington, D.C.: December 1982) and *Standards for Internal Control in the Federal Government* (GAO/AIMD-00-21.3.1, November 1999).

[8] For criteria, see GAO, *2020 Census: Additional Steps Are Needed to Build on Early Planning,* GAO-12-626 (Washington, D.C.: May 17, 2012) and *2010 Census: Cost and Design Issues Need to Be Addressed Soon*, GAO-04-37 (Washington, D.C.: Jan. 15, 2004).

[9] The guides include: A Guide to the Project Management Body of Knowledge, Project Management Institute Standards Committee, @ 1996, Project Management for Mission Critical Systems, a Handbook for Government Executives, Information Technology Resource Board, Apr. 5, 2001, Capability, Maturity Model Integration Project Planning Guide, Carnegie Mellon Software Engineering Institute, March 2001, and U.S. General Accounting Office, Business Process Reengineering Assessment Guide, GAO/AIMD-10.1.15 (Washington, D.C.: May 1997).

[10] In our March 2014 interim report, we defined a large partnership as having 100 or more direct partners and $100 million or more in assets based on IRS data available on direct partners in the Business Returns Transaction File. See GAO-14-379R. We expanded the partner threshold to 100 or more direct and indirect partners after identifying an IRS data source that captures the number of indirect partners, the Enhanced Large Partnership Indicator file. We used the "$100 million or more in assets" threshold because it is consistent with how IRS's annual study of partnership tax returns being filed segregates partnerships by asset size. See IRS Statistics of Income, *Partnership Returns, 2011* (Washington, D.C.: Fall 2013).

[11] IRS's Ogden campus services the IRS's Large Business and International division and field audits of large partnership returns.

[12] Pub. L. No. 97-248, §§ 401–407, 96 Stat. 324, 648–671 (1982). TEFRA established unified audit procedures for covered partnerships and, as amended, are found generally at Internal Revenue Code sections 6221 through 6234. A partnership would fall under the TEFRA audit procedures if at any time during the year it had (1) more than 10 partners or (2) certain types of partners (e.g., another partnership, an LLC that files as a partnership or is treated as a single member, LLC disregarded for federal tax purposes, any type of trust, a nominee, a nonresident alien individual, or a S corporation).

[13] Joint Committee on Taxation, *General Explanation of the Revenue Provisions of the Tax Equity and Fiscal Responsibility Act of 1982*, JCS-38-82, (Washington, D.C.: December 1982).

[14] See U.S. Department of the Treasury, *The President's 1978 Tax Program: Detailed Description and Supporting Analyses of the Proposals*, (Washington, D.C.: Jan. 30, 1978).

[15] See Treasury and IRS, *Widely Held Partnerships: Compliance and Administration Issues – A Report to Congress* (Washington, D.C.: Mar. 30, 1990).

[16] Pub. L. No. 105-34, §§ 1221–1226, 111 Stat. 788, 1006–1020 (1997) (codified at IRC §§ 771–777 and 6240–6242).

[17] ELPs cannot be a partnership engaged in providing services or in buying and selling commodities.

[18] GAO, *Internal Revenue Service: Absorbing Budget Cuts Has Resulted in Significant Staffing Declines and Uneven Performance,* GAO-14-534R (Washington, D.C.: Apr. 21, 2014) and GAO, *IRS 2015 Budget: Long-Term Strategy and Return on Investment Data Needed to Better Manage Budget Uncertainty and Set Priorities*, GAO-14-605 (Washington, D.C.: June 12, 2014)

[19] IRS, "Partnership Returns: Selected Balance Sheet and Income Statement Items, Tax Years 1999-2011, Historical Table 11," Statistics of Income (SOI) Bulletin, http://www.irs.gov/uac/SOI-Tax-Stats-Historical-Table-11 and IRS, "Returns of Active Corporations, Form 1120 and 1120S, Tax Years 2002-2011," Corporation Complete Book, http://www.irs.gov/uac/SOI-Tax-Stats-Corporation-Complete-Report. All estimates derived from samples have 95 percent confidence intervals that are within +/- 10 percentage points of the estimate itself, unless otherwise specified. Calculating percentage changes of numbers presented in above sources may not equal those we present due to rounding.

[20] Similar growth is seen when accounting only for direct partners. Our interim report noted that such large partnerships also more than tripled, from 720 in tax year 2002 to 2,226 in tax year 2011, and total assets increased 200 percent over the same time period to $2.3 trillion. See GAO-14-379R. However, when one partnership has an ownership interest in another, the value of that interest is included in the owner's assets. As a result, assets can be counted more than once in a given population of partnerships, such as both asset numbers we report

above. We do not know the extent to which the large partnerships in our population hold ownership interests in other partnerships, nor do we know how many of those other partnerships may also be large partnerships, so it is unclear how much less these asset data would be if we excluded the presence of assets being counted more than once.

[21] This discussion centers on the number of tiers below a given entity, not the number of tiers above it, because the focus is each large partnership structure. This means that these numbers do not indicate whether a partnership is part of the structure of another pass-through entity and is part of a multitiered network.

[22] According to IRS officials, although it accounts for a vast majority of the large partnerships, the finance and insurance sector represents a small percentage of all partnerships. Among all partnerships in tax year 2011, almost 50 percent were in the real estate, rental, and leasing group, and 9 percent were in the finance and insurance sector. See IRS Statistics of Income, *Partnership Returns, 2011*, (Washington, D.C.: Fall 2013).

[23] See GAO-14-746T. Hedge funds and private equity funds are generally available only to institutions and individuals able to invest in excess of $200,000. Aside from the fund managers, who guide the investment strategy and are general partners, the funds' partners would be comprised of these investors who contributed capital but have no say in investment or management decisions and are the limited partners. See Congressional Research Service, *Taxation of Hedge Fund and Private Equity Managers,* RS22689 (Washington, D.C.: Mar. 7, 2014).

[24] IRS defines the audit rate as the number of returns audited in a fiscal year as a percentage of returns filed in the previous calendar year. In calendar year 2011, there were 10,143 large partnership returns filed. For fiscal year 2013, we did not have 2012 calendar year filings at the time of our analysis to be able to compute the audit coverage rate. This 0.8 percent audit rate excluded campus audits because they are not audits of the books and records of large partnerships, or the returns of the related partners, according to IRS officials. If we included campus audits, the audit rate would inflate to 4 percent. IRS includes campus audits in its counts of all partnership audits in publicly available audit data (IRS, *Data Book 2013*, Publication 55B, Washington, D.C.: March 2014).

[25] GAO-14-379R.

[26] For taxable entities, such as corporations, changes to net income may result in additional recommended tax liability in the form of additional taxes, penalties, or changes to refundable credits. For pass-through entities, such as large partnerships, changes to net income are changes to the entities' reported income, losses, deductions, or credits reflected on the return or the partners' Schedule(s) K-1.

[27] GAO/AIMD-00-21.3.1.

[28] These activity codes focus on whether a partnership reported having less or more than 11 partners as well as reported gross receipts above or below $100,000. IRS also has two activity codes for partnerships that pay an entity level tax at the end of an IRS audit, and that had returns processed prior to January 1988.

[29] According to IRS officials, these limitations are not restricted to audits of large partnerships.

[30] *See Financial Derivatives: Disparate Tax Treatment and Information Gaps Create Uncertainty and Potential Abuse,* GAO-11-750 (Washington, D.C.: Sept. 20, 2011). For more recent information on hedge funds' involvement, see U.S. Senate, Permanent Subcommittee on Investigations, *Abuse of Structured Financial Products: Misusing Basket Options to Avoid Taxes and Leverage Limits*, (Washington, D.C.: July 22, 2014).

[31] In some cases, a taxpayer may agree to extend the statute; however, from fiscal year 2007 through fiscal year 2013, 10 or fewer field audits were granted an extension of the statute of limitations each year.

[32] TMPs have very limited settlements powers under IRC § 6224(c)(3) and may only bind certain partners that have less than a 1 percent interest in the partnership for partnerships that have more than 100 partners. A partner can be a TMP only if that partner was a general partner at some time during the tax year for which the designation was made or was a general partner at the time the designation was made. Additionally, the TMP must be a U.S. person unless no U.S. person meets the TMP qualifications or IRS consents to a foreign TMP. 26 C.F.R. § 301.6231(a)(7)-1(b).

[33] I.R.C. § 6231(a)(7).

[34] See Internal Revenue Manual, section 4.31.2.2.5.1.

[35] IRS has defined the withdrawal period as 45 days in the TEFRA regulations. 26 C.F.R. § 301.6223(a)-2(a).

[36] The regulation specifies that the 45-day rule starts when IRS notifies the TMP of the partnership audit, which likely occurs after the audit start date. However, IRS does not track this notification date. Thus, we counted how many audits closed within 45 days of the audit start date as a proxy.

[37] *See* GAO-14-453.

[38] IRC § 704(b) provides partnerships the option to use special allocations. They are generally listed in the partnership agreement that specifies such things as the partnership's name and purpose, partner contributions, and management responsibilities. The agreement is to specify ratios for passing through partnership income, losses, deductions, and credits to the partners.

[39] Only 15 ELPs had 100 or more direct partners and $100 million or more in assets in tax year 2011.

[40] The Chairman of the House of Representatives Committee on Ways and Means's proposal would apply to partnerships with more than 100 direct partners, or if any partner is itself a partnership. See Joint Committee on Taxation (JCT), Technical Explanation of the Tax Reform Act of 2014, A Discussion Draft of the Chairman of the House Committee on Ways and Means To Reform the Internal Revenue Code Title III – Business Tax Reform, JCX-14-14, (Washington, D.C.: Feb. 26, 2014). The Administration's proposal would apply to partnerships with 1,000 or more direct and indirect partners. See U.S. Department of the Treasury, *General Explanations of the Administration's Fiscal Year 2015 Revenue Proposals*, (Washington, D.C.: March 2014).

[41] TEFRA Coordinators support field audit team with a number of the administrative steps required by TEFRA, such as qualifying the TMP and closing an audit within 45 days.

[42] IRS Strategic Plan: FY2014-2017 (Washington, D.C.: 2014).

[43] See GAO-14-534R.

[44] We have previously identified five principles for effective project planning. See GAO-04-37 and GAO-12-626.

[45] The metrics, which are also used in assessing other audits, are: (1) audit adjustment per staff hour, (2) average months spent on a case, (3) pre-conference hours as a percentage of total case time, (4) total indirect hours as a percentage of total case time, and (5) no change rates. IRS officials also said that they will not be able to determine the effectiveness of changes being tested by the CMT pilot team until the selected returns in the pilot have been audited. As of April 2014, the team projected that these audits would take 18 more months to complete.

[46] See GAO, *Risk Management: Further Refinements Needed to Assess Risks and Prioritize Protective Measures at Ports and Other Critical Infrastructure,* GAO-06-91 (Washington, D.C.: Dec. 15, 2005) and *Patient Protection and Affordable Care Act: IRS Managing Implementation Risks, but Its Approach Could Be Refined,* GAO-12-690 (Washington, D.C.: June 13, 2012).

End Notes for Appendix I

[1] GAO, *Large Partnerships: Characteristics of Population and IRS Audits,* GAO-14-379R (Washington, D.C.: Mar. 19, 2014).

[2] IRS compiles and reports data from audits by predefined codes, known as activity codes. While IRS segregates its corporate audits by activity codes for the corporation's reported asset size, IRS does not segregate its audits of partnerships in this manner and the codes are generally less granulated than those that exist for corporations. As a result, IRS's activity codes do not have a category for "large partnerships." Therefore, to identify the population of large partnership returns subject to IRS audit, we had to merge data in ELPI and BRTF to data AIMS. Since we only identified the population of large partnerships in ELPI and BRTF going back to 2002, the data we report from AIMS on the audited population of returns do not include returns that were filed before 2002. For example, if a return was filed prior to 2002 and then audited by IRS during fiscal years 2007 to 2013, it would not be included in the data we report. We report information on a fiscal-year basis because IRS reports its tax enforcement information on a fiscal year basis in its annual data book. See IRS, *Data Book 2013*, Publication 55B (Washington, D.C.: March 2014). The fiscal year in which the audit is closed is not necessarily representative of the audit activity levels or the audit results for the year of the closure. In many cases, the audits were initiated and the majority of the audit work was done in prior years.

[3] Our recent report and testimony on large partnerships highlighted their growth and the challenges IRS faces in auditing these entities. See GAO, *Large Partnerships: Characteristics of Population and IRS Audits,* GAO-14-379R (Washington, D.C.: Mar. 19, 2014) and *Large Partnerships: Growing Population and Complexity Hinder Effective IRS Audits,* GAO-14-746T (Washington, D.C.: July 22, 2014). For details about all partnerships, see GAO, *Partnerships and S Corporations: IRS Needs to Improve Information to Address Tax Noncompliance,* GAO-14-453 (Washington, D.C.: May 14, 2014).

[4] NVivo is a qualitative data analysis software system that allows organization and analysis of information from a variety of sources including complex nonnumeric or unstructured data.

[5] Pub. L. No. 97-248, §§ 401–407, 96 Stat. 324, 648–671 (1982) and JCT, *General Explanation of the Revenue Provisions of the Tax Equity and Fiscal Responsibility Act of 1982*, JCS-38-82, (Washington, D.C.. December 1982).

[6] GAO/AIMD-00-21.3.1.

[7] GAO, *2020 Census: Additional Steps Are Needed to Build on Early Planning,* GAO-12-626 (Washington, D.C.: May 17, 2012) and *2010 Census: Cost and Design Issues Need to Be Addressed Soon*, GAO-04-37 (Washington, D.C.: Jan. 15, 2004).

[8] The guides include: A Guide to the Project Management Body of Knowledge, Project Management Institute Standards Committee, @ 1996, Project Management for Mission Critical Systems, a Handbook for Government Executives, Information Technology Resource Board, April 5, 2001, Capability, Maturity Model Integration Project Planning

Guide, Carnegie Mellon Software Engineering Institute, March 2001, and U.S. General Accounting Office, Business Process Reengineering Assessment Guide, GAO/AIMD-10.1.15 (Washington, D.C.: May 1997).

In: Large Partnerships
Editor: Francis E. Stephens
ISBN: 978-1-63463-725-1

Chapter 2

LARGE PARTNERSHIPS: CHARACTERISTICS OF POPULATION AND IRS AUDITS*

U.S. Government Accountability Office

The Honorable Ron Wyden
Chairman
Committee on Finance
United States Senate

The Honorable Carl Levin
Chairman

The Honorable John McCain
Ranking Member
Permanent Subcommittee on Investigations
Committee on Homeland Security and Governmental Affairs
United States Senate

In recent years, the number of businesses organized as partnerships has increased significantly, rising 47 percent between tax years 2002 and 2011.[1] In tax year 2011, nearly 3.3 million partnerships accounted for $20.6 trillion in assets and $580.9 billion in total net income.[2] Also from 2002 to 2011, large

* This is an edited, reformatted and augmented version of The United States Government Accountability Office publication, GAO-14-379R, dated March 19, 2014.

partnerships—measured in terms of asset size and number of direct partners[3]—increased significantly as well.[4] Between those tax years, large partnerships (with 100 or more direct partners and $100 million or more in assets) increased more than 200 percent, accounting for $2.3 trillion in total assets and $69.1 billion in total net income by tax year 2011. As the size and number of these large partnerships has grown, Congress and others have raised concerns about the extent to which the Internal Revenue Service (IRS) is able to audit these entities and minimize compliance risk.

Due to the growth of large partnerships and the limited publicly-available data on them, it was requested that we provide information on the number and characteristics of large partnerships and on those large partnership returns that have been subject to IRS audit. Specifically, this report describes (1) the number and characteristics of large partnerships, and (2) the number of IRS audits of large partnership returns and the characteristics of those audits.

This is an interim report; it will contribute to a broader body of work we are conducting on large partnerships and any risks related to their tax compliance. The graphics and data in this report provide a high level overview of the population of large partnerships and of those large partnership returns that have been audited by IRS. Our broader, ongoing work on large partnerships will provide a more in-depth analysis of such IRS data; it will explore why certain differences in the data exist, especially for data pertaining to the audited population of large partnership returns. Our ongoing work will also identify the challenges that auditing large partnership returns presents to IRS and evaluate various actions IRS is taking, both to address those challenges and to reduce the overall risk these entities may present to tax compliance.

For purposes of this report, we did not identify a statutory, IRS, or industry-accepted definition of a large partnership. Instead, we defined "large partnership" using a combination of criteria for partner size and asset size used by IRS. We defined large partnerships as those that reported having 100 or more direct partners[5] and $100 million or more in assets[6] on their Form 1065, U.S. Return of Partnership Income, or on Form 1065-B, U.S. Return of Income for Electing Large Partnerships.[7] A partnership may have qualified for this asset size threshold if it had an ownership interest in another partnership, meaning double counting of assets may exist among this population.[8]

In addition, IRS compiles and reports data from audits by predefined codes, known as activity codes. While IRS segregates its corporate audits by activity codes for the corporation's reported asset size, IRS does not segregate its audits of partnerships in this manner and the codes are generally less granulated than those that exist for corporations. As a result, IRS's activity codes do not have a category for "large partnerships."[9] Therefore, to identify the population of large partnership returns subject to IRS audit, we had to merge certain databases as described below.

To determine the number and characteristics of large partnerships, we obtained data from the Business Return Transaction File (BRTF) on the number and characteristics of large partnerships that filed a Form 1065 or a 1065-B for tax years 2002 through 2011.[10] We analyzed and reported BRTF data by the total number of partnerships that met these criteria during tax years 2002 to 2011. Over the same period of time, we analyzed the number of partnerships by asset and partner size brackets, by average partner and asset size, and by industry group. For figures that were developed as a result of our work on the number and characteristics of large partnerships, see enclosure I.

To determine the number of IRS audits of large partnership returns and the characteristics of those audits, we identified the population of large partnerships in BRTF for tax years 2002 to 2011 and merged that identified population with data from the Audit Information Management System (AIMS).[11] We then used the data to identify and report those partnership returns subject to IRS audit that were closed during fiscal years 2007 to 2013.[12] Once we identified the audited population of large partnership returns, we broke out the results between those audits that were traditional IRS field audits (in which IRS audited the books and records of a partnership return), and campus function audits (in which IRS usually passed audit adjustments through to the related partners' returns).[13] We included campus function audits in our analysis to ensure consistency with IRS, as they include campus function audits when calculating audit coverage rates. We reported the number of audits completed by asset and partner size brackets. We also reported the audit results consistent with how IRS measures them, such as the audit coverage rate (partnership returns subject to audit as a percentage of the total partnership return population) and no change rate (those audits that resulted in no change to the tax return from the audit). Where data were available, we compared these measures for large partnership return audits to those listed in the *IRS Data Book* for corporate return audits of the same asset size.[14] The average values we report in both objectives may be affected disproportionally by a few large outliers as the number of partnerships with 100 or more direct partners and $100 million or more in assets and those that have been audited by IRS are relatively small. For figures and tables that were developed as a result of our work on IRS's audits of large partnership returns, see enclosure II. Where applicable, we noted IRS's comments below each figure and table in enclosures I and II.

For the purposes of this review, we determined that the data from BRTF, AIMS, and the *IRS Data Book* used in our analyses were reliable. Our data reliability assessment included reviewing relevant documentation, conducting interviews with knowledgeable IRS officials, and conducting electronic testing of the data to identify obvious errors or outliers.

We conducted this performance audit from January 2014 to March 2014 in accordance with generally accepted government auditing standards. Those standards require that we plan and perform the audit to obtain sufficient, appropriate evidence to provide a reasonable basis for our findings and conclusions based on our audit objectives. We believe that the evidence obtained provides a reasonable basis for our findings and conclusions based on our audit objectives.

In summary, the number of large partnerships with 100 or more direct partners and $100 million or more in assets increased from 720 in tax year 2002 to 2,226 in tax year 2011. Large partnerships also increased in terms of the average number of direct partners and average asset size. IRS had data on two categories of large partnership return audits. First, the number of completed field audits of large partnership returns increased from 11 in fiscal year 2007 to 31 in fiscal year 2013. Second, IRS counted audits closed through its campus function, which increased from 42 to 143 over the same period. Unlike field audits, campus function audits generally do not entail a review of the books and records of the large partnership return but rather were opened to pass through large partnership return audit adjustments to the related partners' returns. The percentage of IRS audits that resulted in no change to the taxpayer's return varied from fiscal year 2007 to 2013 but was 52 percent for campus function audits and 45 percent for field audits in fiscal year 2013.

AGENCY COMMENTS

We provided a draft of this report to the Secretary of the Treasury and the Commissioner of Internal Revenue for comment. IRS provided technical comments that we incorporated, as appropriate. Treasury had no comments.

James R. White Director,
Tax Issues
Strategic Issues

ENCLOSURE I: NUMBER AND CHARACTERISTICS OF LARGE PARTNERSHIP RETURNS

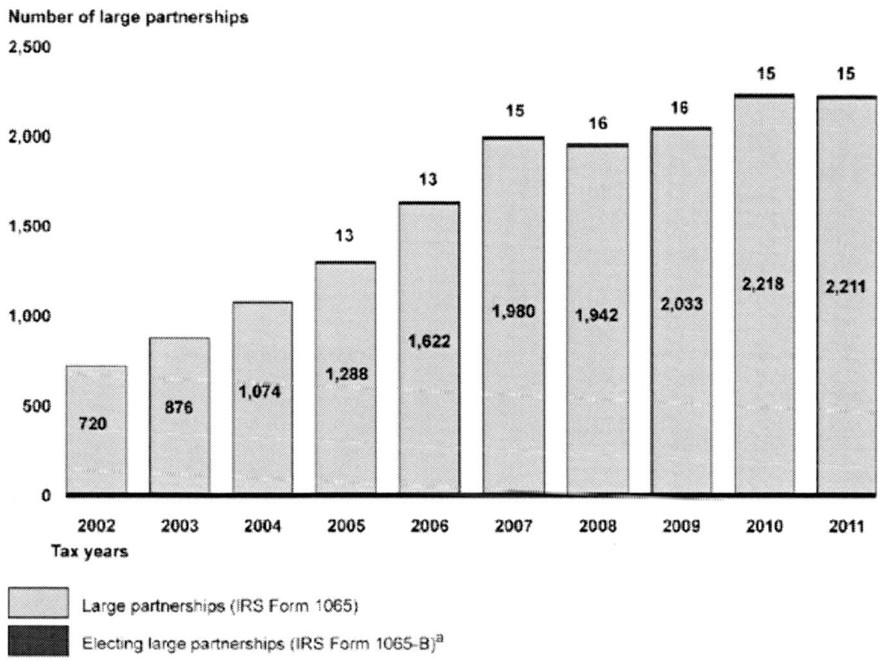

Source: GAO analysis of IRS data from Business Return Transaction File (BRTF), Compliance Data Warehouse (CDW).

Notes: This figure only includes data on partnerships that reported 100 or more direct partners and $100 million or more in assets on their Form 1065 or 1065-B.

[a] Large partnerships may choose to elect into an alternative IRS reporting and auditing process that uses a Form 1065-B to report annual partnership tax information. These entities are known as electing large partnerships. To make the election, the partnership must have had 100 or more direct partners during the preceding tax year. (To avoid disclosure of information about specific taxpayers, electing large partnership values for 2002 to 2004 are not shown.)

Figure 1. Large Partnerships by Form 1065 and 1065-B Tax Returns, Tax Years 2002 to 2011.

> *IRS comments*: Only 15 electing large partnerships had $100 million or more in assets in tax year 2011. (For context, there were 105 partnerships that filed a Form 1065-B in tax year 2011. See IRS Statistics of Income, *Partnership Returns, 2011* (Washington, D.C.: Fall 2013)

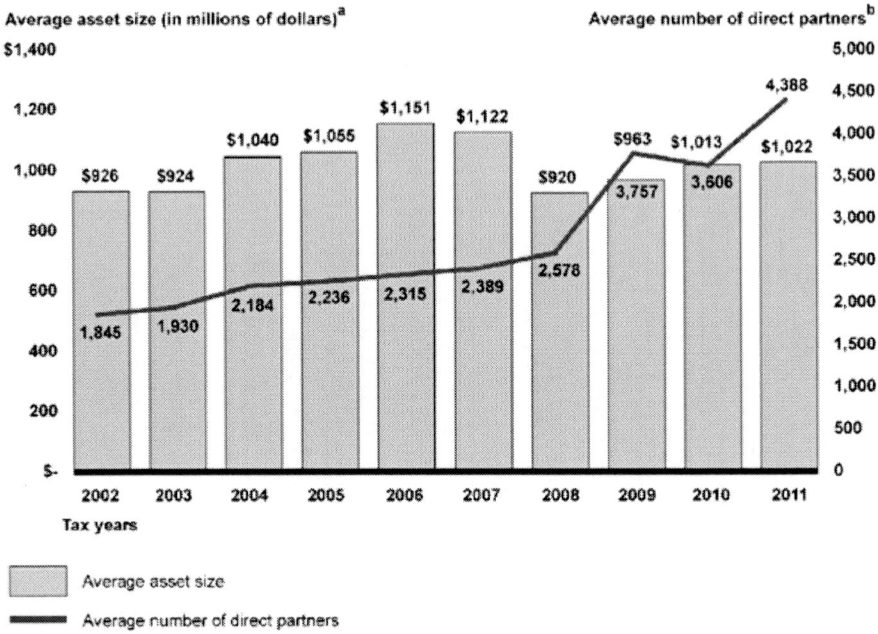

Source: GAO analysis of IRS data from Business Return Transaction File (BRTF), Compliance Data Warehouse (CDW).

Notes: This figure only includes data on partnerships that reported 100 or more direct partners and $100 million or more in assets on their Form 1065.

[a] Some of the large partnerships may not have reached the $100 million asset threshold without their ownership interests in other partnerships. The average asset size is also higher than it would be without those ownership interests.

[b] Direct partners are those partners that have a direct interest in the large partnership during the tax year and are reported on Form 1065 or Form 1065-B.

Figure 2. Large Partnerships (Form 1065) by Average Asset Size and Number of Direct Partners, Tax Years 2002 to 2011.

IRS comments: The drop in the average asset size in 2008 may have been due to the economic recession.

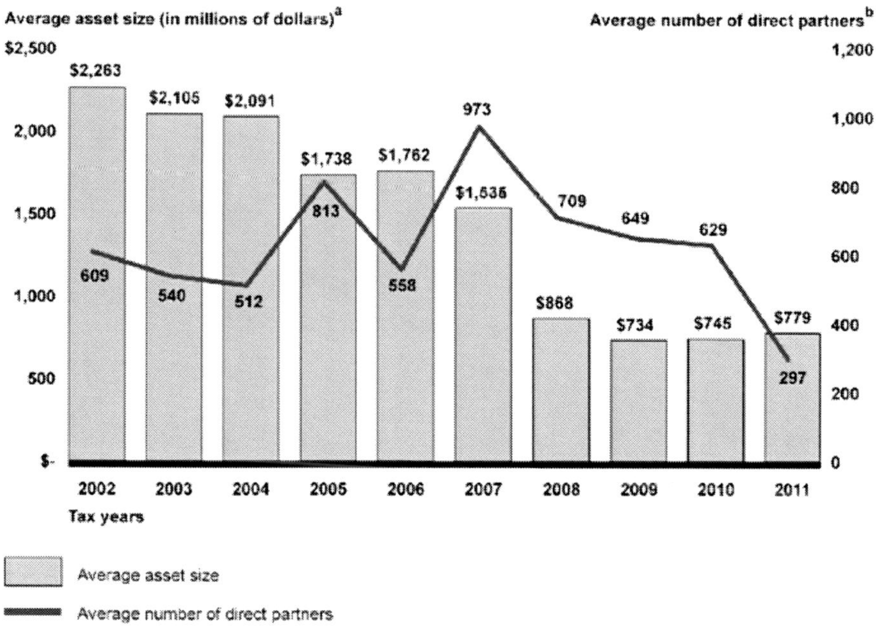

Source: GAO analysis of IRS data from Business Return Transaction File (BRTF), Compliance Data Warehouse (CDW).

Notes: This figure only includes data on those partnerships that reported 100 or more direct partners and $100 million or more in assets on their Form 1065-B. Large partnerships may choose to elect into an alternative IRS reporting and auditing process that uses a Form 1065-B to report annual partnership tax information. These entities are known as electing large partnerships. To make the election, the partnership must have had 100 or more direct partners during the preceding tax year.

[a] Some of the large partnerships may not have reached the $100 million asset threshold without their ownership interests in other partnerships. The average asset size is also higher than it would be without those ownership interests.

[b] Direct partners are those partners that have a direct interest in the large partnership during the tax year and are reported on Form 1065 or Form 1065-B.

Figure 3. Electing Large Partnerships (Form 1065-B) by Average Asset Size and Number of Direct Partners, Tax Years 2002 to 2011.

IRS comments: The drop in the average asset size in 2008 may have been due to the economic recession.

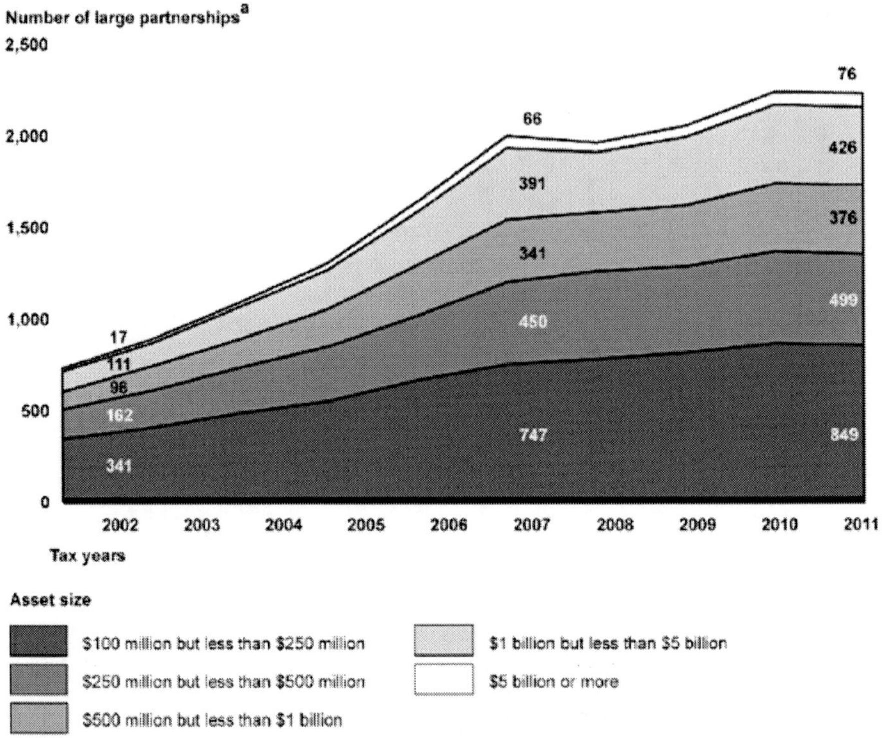

Source: GAO analysis of IRS data from Business Return Transaction File (BRTF), Compliance Data Warehouse (CDW).

Notes: This figure only includes data on partnerships that reported 100 or more direct partners and $100 million or more in assets on their Form 1065 or 1065-B.

[a] Some of the large partnerships may not have reached the $100 million asset threshold without their ownership interests in other partnerships. The average asset size is also higher than it would be without those ownership interests.

Figure 4. Large Partnerships by Asset Size, Tax Years 2002 to 2011.

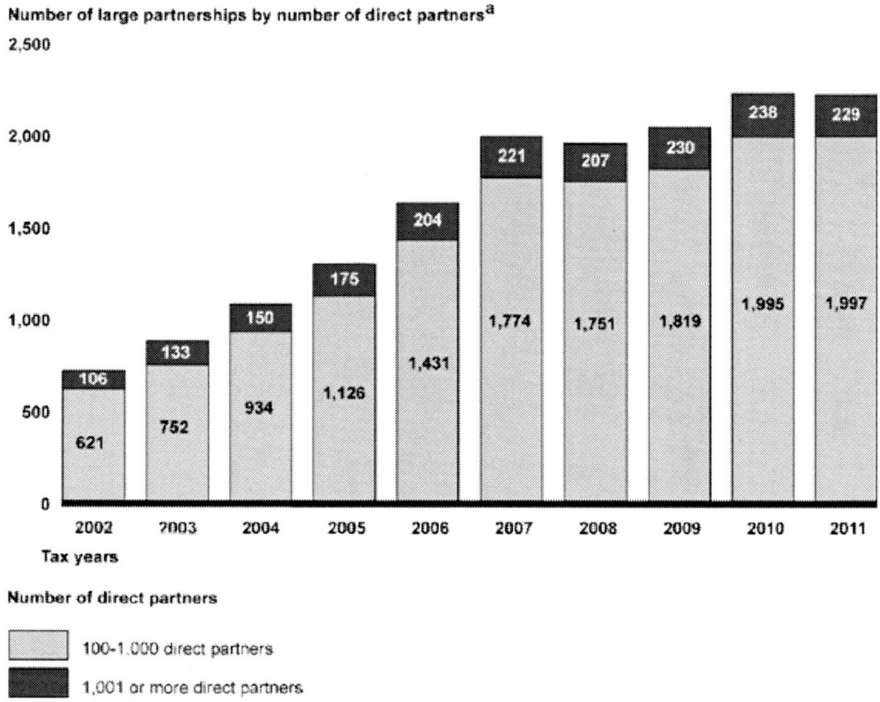

Source: GAO analysis of IRS data from Business Return Transaction File (BRTF), Compliance Data Warehouse (CDW).

Notes: This figure only includes data on partnerships that reported 100 or more direct partners and $100 million or more in assets on their Form 1065 or 1065-B.

The direct partner break point of 1,000 for figure 5 was used as it is consistent with the threshold used by one IRS initiative under way to identify large partnerships as well as a legislative proposal for auditing large partnerships. We will discuss both of these further in our broader work on large partnerships.

[a] Direct partners are those partners that have a direct interest in the large partnership during the tax year and are reported on Form 1065 or1065-B.

Figure 5. Large Partnerships by Number of Direct Partners, Tax Years 2002 to 2011.

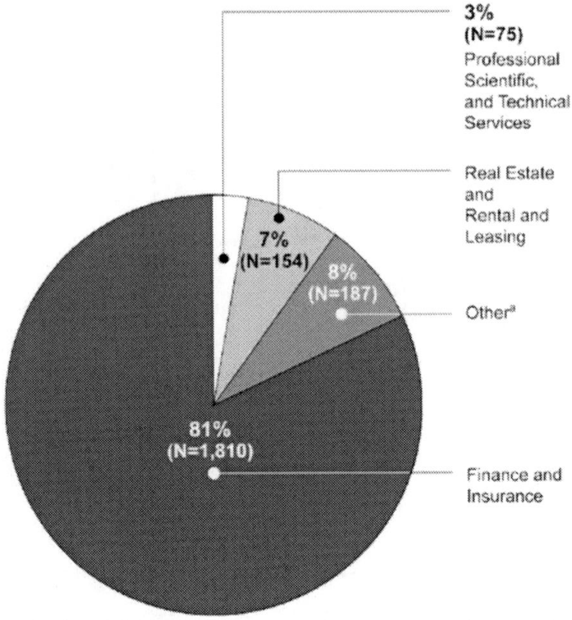

Source: GAO analysis of IRS data from Business Return Transaction File (BRTF), Compliance Data Warehouse (CDW).

Notes: This figure only includes data on partnerships that reported 100 or more direct partners and $100 million or more in assets on their Form 1065 or 1065-B. Results from tax year 2011 are generally consistent with average distribution of large partnerships by industry from tax years 2002 to 2011. Industry group percentages may not sum to 100 percent due to rounding.

[a] "Other" includes the following industry groups: agriculture, forestry, fishing and hunting; mining; utilities; construction; wood product manufacturing; primary metal manufacturing; wholesale trade; retail trade; sporting goods, hobby, book, and music stores; transportation and warehousing; couriers and messengers; information; management of companies (holding companies); health care and social assistance; arts, entertainment, and recreation; accommodation and food services; and other services. Industry classifications are based on the North American Industry Classification System (NAICS). NAICS codes are self-reported by businesses and may involve a certain amount of judgment to determine the most appropriate NAICS code.

Figure 6. Large Partnerships by Industry Group, Tax Year 2011.

IRS comments: Although it accounts for a vast majority of the large partnerships, the Finance and Insurance group tends to account for a small percentage among all types of partnerships whereas the Real Estate and Rental group tends to account for a larger percentage.

(For context, among all partnerships in tax year 2011, almost 50 percent were in the Real Estate and Rental and Leasing group and 9 percent were in the Finance and Insurance group. See IRS Statistics of Income, *Partnership Returns, 2011*, Washington, D.C.: Fall 2013.)

ENCLOSURE II: NUMBER OF IRS AUDITS OF LARGE PARTNERSHIP RETURNS AND THE CHARACTERISTICS OF THOSE AUDITS

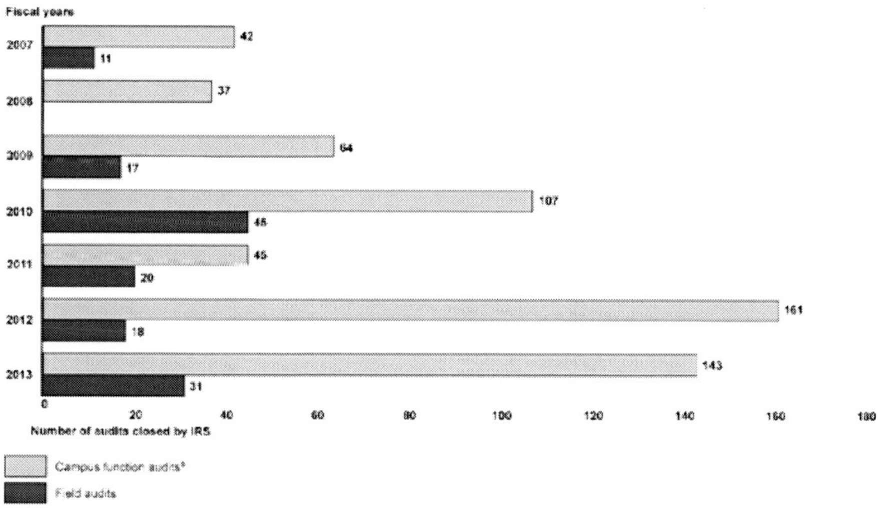

Source: GAO analysis of IRS data from Audit Information Mamagement System (AIMS), Compliance Data Warehouse (CDW).

Notes: For audits closed in a particular year, IRS uses codes that predefine certain audited populations by fiscal year, known as activity codes. For example, all corporate audits can be segregated by codes for a corporation's reported asset size; however, audits of partnership returns are currently not segregated in this manner and the codes are generally less granulated than those that exist for corporations. As a result, IRS's activity codes do not have a category for "large partnerships." Therefore, in order to identify the population of large partnership returns subject to IRS audit, we had to merge certain databases, which presented certain data limitations (as identified previously). The number of audits closed in a given fiscal year may include multiple returns of the same taxpayer from different tax years that were closed in the same fiscal year.

This figure only includes data on partnership returns audited by IRS that reported 100 or more direct partners and $100 million or more in assets on their Form 1065 or

1065-B. However, no partnerships that filed a Form 1065-B from tax years 2002 to 2011 had their tax return audited and closed by IRS from fiscal years 2007 to 2013. To avoid disclosure of information about specific taxpayers, the field audit value for 2008 is not shown.

[a] Campus function audits are mainly an administrative support function used by IRS. While technically those audits opened in the campus function are considered audits by IRS, they generally do not entail a review of the books and records of the taxpayer return in question, in contrast to audits completed in the field. Although the number is not known, IRS officials noted that a small number of field audits are transferred and are closed as campus audits because of open audits at the campus of related returns.

Figure 7. Audits of Large Partnership Returns Closed by IRS by Type of Audit, Fiscal Years 2007 to 2013.

Table 1. Audits of Large Partnership Returns Closed by IRS by Type of Audit and Asset Size, Fiscal Year 2013

	Asset size		
	$100 million tounder $1 billion	$1 billion or more	Total
Type of audit	Number of audits		
IRS campus function audits[a]	103	40	143
IRS field audits	17	14	31
Total IRS large partnership audits	120	54	174

Source: GAO analysis of IRS data from Audit Information Management System (AIMS), Compliance Data Warehouse (CDW).

Notes: This figure only includes data on partnership returns audited by IRS that reported 100 or more direct partners and $100 million or more in assets on their Form 1065 or 1065-B. However, no partnerships that filed a Form 1065-B from tax years 2002 to 2011 had their tax return audited and closed by IRS from fiscal years 2007 to 2013. The number of audits closed in a given fiscal year may include multiple returns of the same taxpayer from different tax years that were closed in the same fiscal year.

Some of the large partnerships may not have reached the $100 million asset threshold without their ownership interests in other partnerships. The average asset size is also higher than it would be without those ownership interests.

[a]Campus function audits are mainly an administrative support function used by IRS. While technically those audits opened in the campus function are considered audits by IRS, they generally do not entail a review of the books and records of the taxpayer return in question, in contrast to audits completed in the field. Although the number is not known, IRS officials noted that a small number of field audits are transferred and are closed as campus audits because of open audits at the campus of related returns.

Table 2. Audits of Large Partnership Returns Closed by IRS by Audit Type and Number of Direct Partners, Fiscal Year 2013

	Number of direct partners[a]		
	100 tounder 201 direct partners	201 or more direct partners	Total
Type of audit	Number of audits		
IRS campus function audits[b]	63	80	143
IRS field audits	15	16	31
Total IRS large partnership audits	78	96	174

Source: GAO analysis of IRS data from Audit Information Management System (AIMS), Compliance Data Warehouse (CDW).

Notes: This figure only includes data on partnership returns audited by IRS that reported 100 or more direct partners and $100 million or more in assets on their Form 1065 or 1065-B. However, no partnerships that filed a Form 1065-B from tax years 2002 to 2011 had their tax return audited and closed by IRS from fiscal years 2007 to 2013. The number of audits closed in a given fiscal year may include multiple returns of the same taxpayer from different tax years that were closed in the same fiscal year.

The direct partner break point of 200 for table 2 differs from that of figure 5 because we had to consolidate counts of audits of partnership returns to avoid disclosure of information about specific taxpayers.

[a] Direct partners are those partners that have a direct interest in the large partnership during the tax year and are reported on Form 1065 or Form 1065-B. Beyond the number of direct partners, the campus function also would pass through the adjustments from auditing a large partnership to any indirect partners, including another partnership.

[b] Campus function audits are mainly an administrative support function used by IRS. While technically those audits opened in the campus function are considered audits by IRS, they generally do not entail a review of the books and records of the taxpayer return in question, in contrast to audits completed in the field. Although the number is not known, IRS officials noted that a small number of field audits are transferred and are closed as campus audits because of open audits at the campus of related returns.

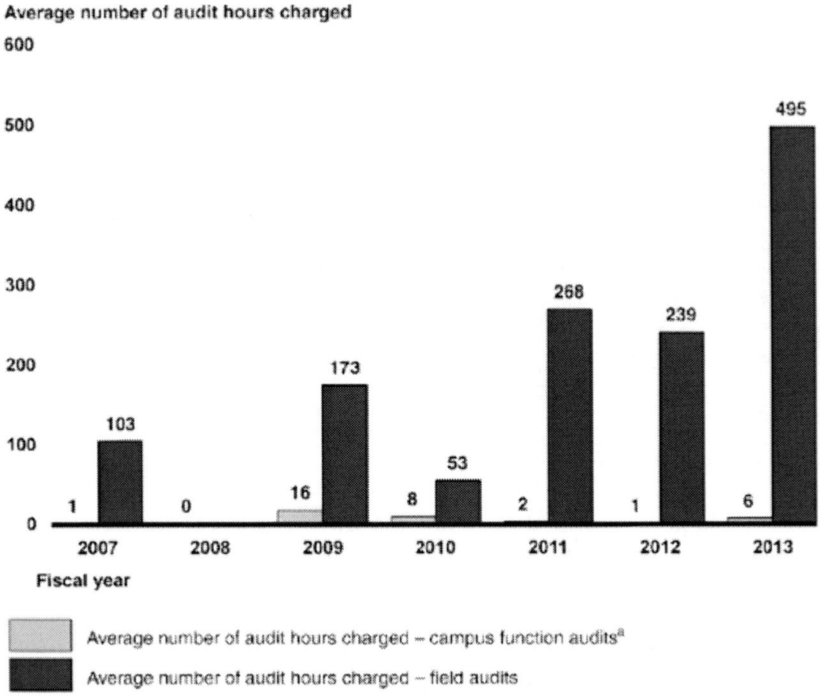

Source: GAO analysis of IRS data from Audit Information Mamagement System (AIMS), Compliance Data Warehouse (CDW).

Notes: This figure only includes data on partnership returns audited by IRS that reported 100 or more direct partners and $100 million or more in assets on their Form 1065 or 1065-B. However, no partnerships that filed a Form 1065-B from tax years 2002 to 2011 had their tax return audited and closed by IRS from fiscal years 2007 to 2013. To avoid disclosure of information about specific taxpayers, the field audit value for 2008 is not shown.

[a] Campus function audits are mainly an administrative support function used by IRS. While technically those audits opened in the campus function are considered audits by IRS, they generally do not entail a review of the books and records of the taxpayer return in question, in contrast to audits completed in the field. Although the number is not known, IRS officials noted that a small number of field audits are transferred and are closed as campus audits because of open audits at the campus of related returns.

Figure 8. Average IRS Hours Charged on Audits of Large Partnership Returns by Audit Type, Fiscal Years 2007 to 2013.

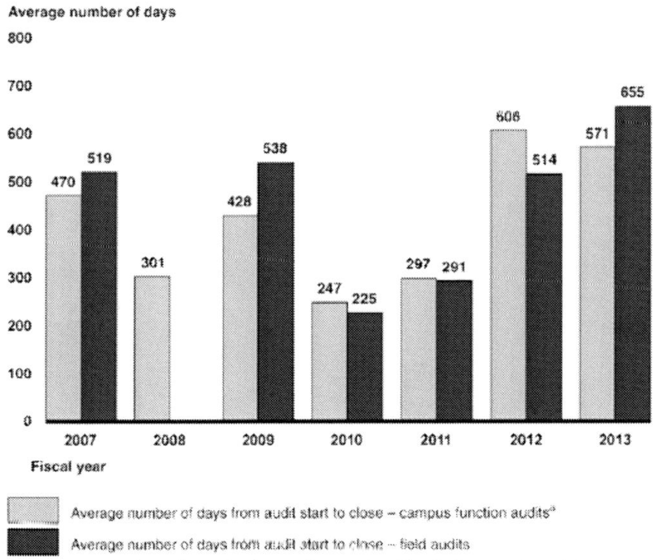

Source: GAO analysis of IRS data from Audit Information Management System (AIMS), Compliance Data Warehouse (CDW).

Notes: This figure only includes data on partnership returns audited by IRS that reported 100 or more direct partners and $100 million or more in assets on their Form 1065 or 1065-B. However, no partnerships that filed a Form 1065-B from tax years 2002 to 2011 had their tax return audited and closed by IRS from fiscal years 2007 to 2013. To avoid disclosure of information about specific taxpayers, the field audit value for 2008 is not shown.

[a] Campus function audits are mainly an administrative support function used by IRS. While technically those audits opened in the campus function are considered audits by IRS, they generally do not entail a review of the books and records of the taxpayer return in question, in contrast to audits completed in the field. Although the number is not known, IRS officials noted that a small number of field audits are transferred and are closed as campus audits because of open audits at the campus of related returns.

Figure 9. Average Number of Days That Audits of Large Partnership Returns Were Open at IRS by Type of Audit, Fiscal Years 2007 to 2013.

IRS comments: Campus function audits may take longer than field audits. The campus creates a package of returns linked to the field audit of a large partnership shortly after the field begins its work. These returns remain open in the campus until adjustments from the field audit can be passed through the linked returns. In addition, partner returns can be held in suspense for years if the partnership return ends up in court. While the field will count their partnership return audit as closed, the related partner returns may not close for years. The time in suspense on those cases will skew the data significantly considering partner returns from the late 1980s and early 1990s are still in suspense awaiting court decisions.

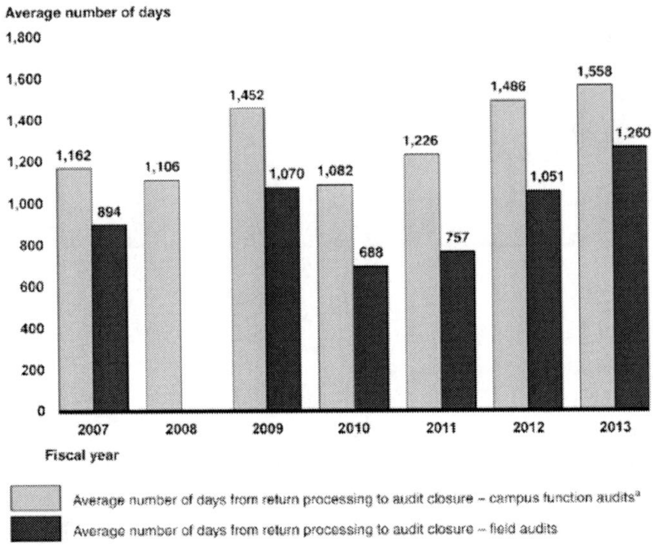

Source: GAO analysis of IRS data from Audit Information Mamagement System (AIMS), Compliance Data Warehouse (CDW).

Notes: The average number of days from return posting to audit closure represents the average number of days from when a return is processed and posted to its IRS account until the return was closed from an audit. This figure only includes data on partnership returns audited by IRS that reported 100 or more direct partners and $100 million or more in assets on their Form 1065 or 1065-B. However, no partnerships that filed a Form 1065-B from tax years 2002 to 2011 had their tax return audited and closed by IRS from fiscal years 2007 to 2013. To avoid disclosure of information about specific taxpayers, the field audit value for 2008 is not shown.

[a] Campus function audits are mainly an administrative support function used by IRS. While technically those audits opened in the campus function are considered audits by IRS, they generally do not entail a review of the books and records of the taxpayer return in question, in contrast to audits completed in the field. Although the number is not known, IRS officials noted that a small number of field audits are transferred and are closed as campus audits because of open audits at the campus of related returns.

Figure 10. Average Number of Days from Return Processing to IRS Audit Closure for Audits of Large Partnership Returns by Type of Audit, Fiscal Years 2007 to 2013.

IRS comments: Campus function audits may take longer than field audits. The campus creates a package of returns linked to the field audit of a large partnership shortly after the field begins its work. These returns remain open in the campus until adjustments from the field audit can be passed through the linked returns. In addition, partner returns can be held in suspense for years if the partnership return ends up in court. While the field will count their partnership return audit as closed, the related partner returns may not close for years. The time in suspense on those cases will skew the data significantly considering partner returns from the late 1980s and early 1990s are still in suspense awaiting court decisions.

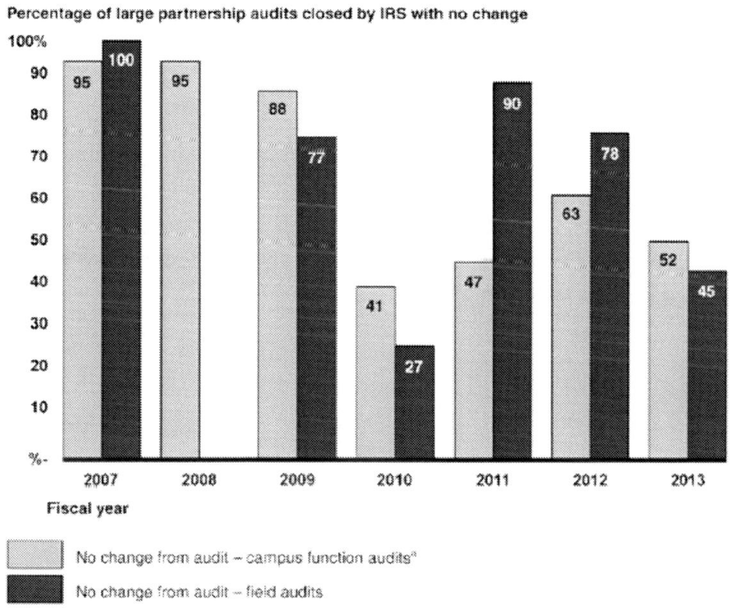

Source: GAO analysis of IRS data from Audit Information Mamagement System (AIMS), Compliance Data Warehouse (CDW).

Notes: For entities, such as partnerships that pass through income to the partners of the business, the no change results from these audits meant that there were no changes made to the entities' reported income, loss, deductions, or credits reflected on the tax return or Schedule(s) K-1 for partners of the partnership. These instances would be included in the no change rate in the figure above. IRS also closes audits if no changes were made to the entities' reported income, loss, deductions, or credits reflected on the tax return or the Schedule(s) K-1 for partners of the partnership but a balance sheet item is adjusted or a related return is adjusted as a result of the audit. These instances are not included in the no change rate in the figure above.

This figure only includes data on partnership returns audited by IRS that reported 100 or more direct partners and $100 million or more in assets on their Form 1065 or 1065-B. However, no partnerships that filed a Form 1065-B from tax years 2002 to 2011 had their tax return audited and closed by IRS from fiscal years 2007 to 2013. To avoid disclosure of information about specific taxpayers, the no change rate from field audit value for 2008 is not shown.

[a] Campus function audits are mainly an administrative support function used by IRS. While technically those audits opened in the campus function are considered audits by IRS, they generally do not entail a review of the books and records of the taxpayer return in question, in contrast to audits completed in the field. Although the number is not known, IRS officials noted that a small number of field audits are transferred and are closed as campus audits because of open audits at the campus of related returns.

Figure 11. No Change Rates for Audits of Large Partnership Returns Closed by IRS, by Type of Audit, Fiscal Years 2007 to 2013.

IRS comments: The drop in the no change rate for campus function audits in 2010 and 2011 reflects a revision made starting in late 2009 in which the campus function revised how no change audits were tracked. The lower no change rates for the campus function in 2010 and 2011 may also be due to a lower no change rate in the field in 2010.

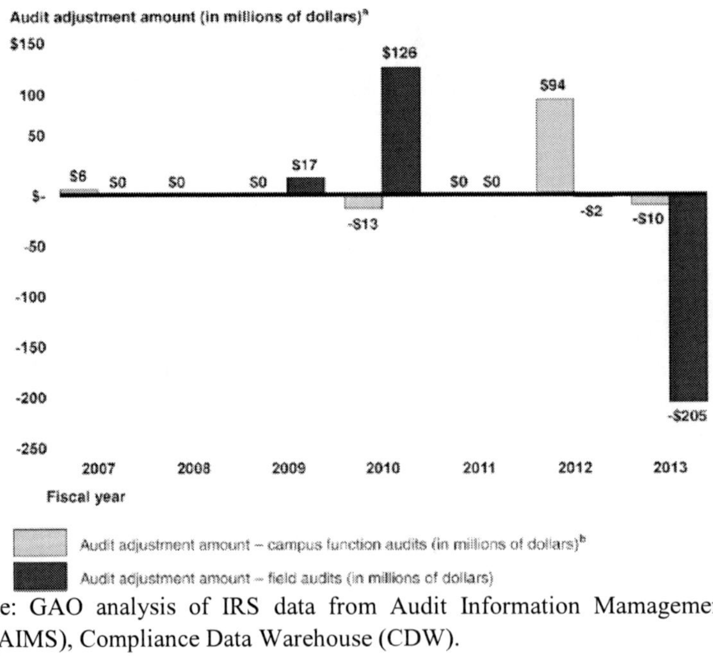

Source: GAO analysis of IRS data from Audit Information Mamagement System (AIMS), Compliance Data Warehouse (CDW).

Notes: This figure only includes data on partnership returns audited by IRS that reported 100 or more direct partners and $100 million or more in assets on their Form 1065 or 1065-B. However, no partnerships that filed a Form 1065-B from tax years 2002 to 2011 had their tax return audited and closed by IRS from fiscal years 2007 to 2013. To avoid disclosure of information about specific taxpayers, the field audit value for 2008 is not shown.

[a] The audit adjustment amount is the net increase or decrease of adjustments made to income, deductions, and other required information items on Form 1065 or 1065-B as the result of an IRS audit.

[b] Campus function audits are mainly an administrative support function used by IRS. While technically those audits opened in the campus function are considered audits by IRS, they generally do not entail a review of the books and records of the taxpayer return in question, in contrast to audits completed in the field. Although the number is not known, IRS officials noted that a small number of field audits are transferred and are closed as campus audits because of open audits at the campus of related returns.

Figure 12. Total Audit Adjustment Amount for Audits of Large Partnership Returns by Type of Audit, Fiscal Years 2007 to 2013.

IRS comments: In general, total audit adjustment amounts only include those to net income rather than changes IRS made to the balance sheet unless the changes ultimately have some tax effect.

Table 3. Audits of Large Partnership Returns as a Percentage of Total Large Partnership Returns by Audit Type and Asset Size, Fiscal Years 2007 to 2012

			Fiscal year			
Large partnership audits by type	*2007*	*2008*	*2009*	*2010*	*2011*	*2012*
IRS campus function audits[a]	2.6%	1.9%	3.3%	5.3%	2.0%	7.1%
IRS field audits	0.7%	d	0.9%	2.2%	0.9%	0.8%
Total large partnerships audits	*3.3%*	*d*	*4.2%*	*7.5%*	*2.9%*	*7.9%*
Large partnership audits by asset size						
$100 million to under $250 million	3.0%	1.9%	4.7%	6.1%	3.0%	7.6%
$250 million to under $500 million	4.3%	2.7%	5.0%	7.1%	3.0%	6.5%
$500 million to under $1 billion	d	d	d	9.5%	3.1%	11.9%
$1 billion or more	4.0%	2.9%	3.7%	9.0%	2.6%	6.8%

Source: GAO analysis of IRS data from Business Return Transaction File (BRTF) and Audit Information Management System (AIMS), Compliance Data Warehouse (CDW).

Legend: d = Value not shown. To avoid disclosure of information about specific taxpayers, audit coverage rate values for the $500 million to under $1 billion asset class for 2007 to 2009 and field audit and total values for 2008 are not shown.

Notes: The audit coverage rate calculations are completed by dividing those partnership returns with $100 million or more in assets and 100 or more direct partners, as reported on Form 1065 or 1065-B (which were audited in the current fiscal year by those returns filed in the previous calendar year). To the extent we changed the partner threshold of 100 or more direct partners, the audit coverage rates above would likely change. However, no partnerships that filed a Form 1065-B from tax years 2002 to 2011 had their tax return audited and closed by IRS from fiscal years 2007 to 2013. These calculations are consistent with how IRS completes audit coverage rate calculations.

The number of audits closed in a given fiscal year may include multiple returns of the same taxpayer from different tax years that were closed in the same fiscal year. The number of returns filed in the previous calendar year would not be adjusted in this case.

For audits closed in a particular year, IRS uses codes that predefine certain audited populations by fiscal year, known as activity codes. For example, all corporate audits can be segregated by codes for a corporation's reported asset size; however, audits of partnership returns are currently not segregated in this manner and the codes are generally less granulated than those that exist for corporations. As a result, IRS's activity codes do not have a category for "large partnerships." Therefore, in order to identify the population of large partnership returns subject to IRS audit, we had to merge certain databases, which presented certain data limitations (as identified previously).

Data reported for partnerships were not available in BRTF at the time of our report in order for us to do the fiscal year 2013 calculation.

[a] Campus function audits are mainly an administrative support function used by IRS. While technically those audits opened in the campus function are considered audits by IRS, they generally do not entail a review of the books and records of the taxpayer return in question, in contrast to audits completed in the field. Although the number is not known, IRS officials noted that a small number of field audits are transferred and are closed as campus audits because of open audits at the campus of related returns.

Table 4. Audits of Large Corporate Returns as a Percentage of Total Large Corporate Returns by Total Population and Asset Size, Fiscal Years 2007 to 2012

			Fiscal year			
Corporation audits by asset size	*2007*	*2008*	*2009*	*2010*	*2011*	*2012*
$100 million or more	21.4%	22.0%	21.3%	21.4%	23.6%	27.1%

			Fiscal year			
Corporation audits by asset size	*2007*	*2008*	*2009*	*2010*	*2011*	*2012*
$100 million to under $250 million	12.1%	12.8%	13.6%	14.7%	16.6%	23.2%
$250 million to under $500 million	14.3%	14.2%	15.8%	16.1%	17.4%	22.7%
$500 million to under $1 billion	18.5%	18.6%	18.1%	18.1%	20.6%	22.7%
$1 billion to under $5 billion	31.6%	31.2%	27.3%	28.6%	31.1%	31.4%
$5 billion to under $20 billion	62.9%	64.2%	48.7%	45.3%	50.5%	45.4%
$20 billion or more	119.5%	127.1%	114.4%	98.0%	95.6%	93.0%

Source: IRS data book.

Notes: Audit coverage rate calculations in the IRS data book are completed by dividing the number of audits of corporate returns completed in the current fiscal year by the number of returns filed in the prior calendar year.

Corporate audit coverage rates are presented to provide context for similar asset size business entities to those presented for partnerships in table 3.

The percentage of returns audited may be greater than 100 percent of the returns filed in the previous calendar year since audits may be conducted in one fiscal year on returns filed in multiple prior calendar years.

The 2013 IRS Data Book was not available at the time of this report; therefore, we could not present the fiscal year 2013 audit rates for corporate returns.

End Notes

[1] A partnership is a "pass-through" or "flow-through" entity for tax purposes because the income earned by partnerships is attributed to (or passed through to) the owners of the business; this income is—in general—taxed only once for partners who are taxable (as is done under the individual income tax system).

[2] Internal Revenue Service, "Partnership Returns: Selected Balance Sheet and Income Statement Items, Tax Years 1999-2011, Historical Table 11," Statistics of Income (SOI) Bulletin, accessed February 18, 2014, http://www.irs.gov/uac/SOI-Tax-Stats-Historical-Table-11.

[3] Direct partners are those partners that have a direct interest in the large partnership during the tax year.

[4] The terms "large partnership" and "large, widely-held partnership" do not have a single, widely accepted definition. The Internal Revenue Code (IRC) does define an electing large partnership as a partnership that had 100 or more direct partners during the preceding tax year and makes an election. Electing large partnerships choose an alternative IRS reporting and auditing process that uses a Form 1065-B to report annual partnership tax information. See 26 U.S.C. § 775(a)(1).

[5] We used the "100 or more direct partners" threshold because it is consistent with the criterion that a partnership must meet to file a Form 1065-B. However, the number of direct partners may not capture the total partner size of a partnership structure if one or more partnerships have an ownership interest in another partnership. For example, a partnership may have few direct partners, but thousands of indirect partners if its direct partners are partnerships themselves, which in turn have a large number of partners.

[6] We used the "$100 million or more in assets" threshold because it is consistent with how IRS's annual partnership study segregates large partnerships by asset size. See IRS Statistics of Income, Partnership Returns, 2011 (Washington, D.C.: Fall 2013).

[7] Every partnership with any item of taxable income, deduction, or credit is required to file a Form 1065 or 1065-B showing these items. Foreign partnerships must do so if they have gross income derived from sources within the United States or gross income effectively connected with the conduct of a trade or business in the United States.

[8] When one partnership has an ownership interest in another, the value of that interest is included in the owner's assets. As a result, double counting of assets can occur in a given population of partnerships. For example, if partnership A owns a 50 percent interest in partnership B, which has total assets of $10 million, then (depending on its accounting method), partnership A's total assets could include $5 million that were also reported as part of partnership B's assets. Some of the large partnerships in our population may not have reached the $100 million asset threshold without their ownership interests in other partnerships. The average asset size of this population is also higher than it would be without those ownership interests. We do not know the extent to which the large partnerships in our population hold ownership interests in other partnerships, nor do we know how many of those other partnerships may also be large partnerships.

[9] The activity codes for partnerships include 480, all partnership returns processed prior to January 1988; 481, 10 or fewer partners with gross receipts under $100,000; 482, 10 or fewer partners with gross receipts of $100,000 or more; and 483, 11 or more partners. Partnerships that pay an entity level tax at the conclusion of an IRS audit, such as an electing large partnership, have an activity code of 473. IRS plans to implement a new activity code structure for partnerships in fiscal year 2015 that would provide a more granulated breakout and allow IRS to report on partnership audit results by various asset sizes. IRS plans to report on this activity code structure beginning in fiscal year 2016.

[10] Return data from tax year 2011 was the most recent year of data available in BRTF.

[11] Since we only identified the population of large partnerships in BRTF going back to 2002, the data we report from AIMS on the audited population of returns does not include returns that were filed before 2002. For example, if a return was filed prior to 2002 and then audited by IRS during fiscal years 2002 to 2013, it would not be included in the data we report. In addition, since there is a time lag from when IRS processes a partnership return to when that return is selected for audit and subsequently closed, we only report data from AIMS on the audited population for fiscal year 2007 to 2013.

[12] We report information on a fiscal year basis because IRS reports its tax enforcement information on a fiscal year basis in its annual data book. See Internal Revenue Service, Data Book 2012, Publication 55B (Washington, D.C.: March 2013). The fiscal year the audit is closed is not necessarily representative of the audit activity levels or the audit results for the year of the closure. In many cases, the audits were initiated and the majority of the audit work was done in prior years.

[13] IRS data includes two types of partnership return audits. A campus function audit is mainly an administrative support function used by IRS. While technically considered to be audits by IRS, campus function audits generally do not entail a review of the books and records of the taxpayer return in question, as do audits completed in the field. IRS staff said that the number of indirect partners of a partnership has more of an impact on IRS's campus function than on the field audits. IRS staff added that partnership returns filed between tax years 2002 and 2011, with between 100 and 1,000 total investors, which include both direct and indirect partners, averaged 44 direct partners. Those with between 1,001 and 100,000

total investors averaged 130 direct partners. IRS said these partnership structures can be very large and that special allocations within each individual partnership, which is a partner of the partnership structure, make it difficult to process the adjustments through to the taxable entities.

[14] The IRS Data Book is only available through 2012, so we report data from fiscal years 2007 to 2012. See Internal Revenue Service, Data Book 2012, Publication 55B (Washington, D.C.: March 2013).

INDEX

E

F

G

H

I

L

M

T

U

V

W